Rollicking Riddles

Rollicking Riddles

1 What has eyes but cannot see?
A potato.

2 What is there more of the less you see?
Darkness.

3 What has eyes that cannot see, a tongue that cannot taste, and a soul that cannot die?
A shoe.

4 What's grey and can't see well from either end?
A donkey with its eyes shut.

5 What can you hear but not see and only speaks when it is spoken to?
An echo.

6 What invention allows you to see through walls?
A window.

7 Which is the longest rope?
Europe.

8 What bet can never be won?
The alphabet.

9 Why did the boy sit on the clock?
He wanted to be on time.

10 What do elephants play marbles with?
Old bowling balls.

11 Why is the Mississippi such an unusual river?
It has four eyes and can't even see.

12 What can be caught and heard but never seen?
A remark.

13 What can you hold without touching?
Your breath.

14 Why should you never tell secrets in a grocery store?
Because the corn has ears, potatoes have eyes and beanstalk.

15 Why is milk the fastest thing in the world?
Because it's pasteurised before you see it.

16 If a butcher is two metres tall and has size 11 feet, what does he weigh?
Meat.

17 What's the same size and shape as an elephant but weighs nothing?
An elephant's shadow.

18 Which candle burns longer, a red one or a green one?
Neither, they both burn shorter.

19 What part of a fish weighs the most?
The scales.

20 What is bigger when it's upside down?
The number 6.

21 What weighs more, a kilo of lead or a kilo of feathers?
They both weigh the same.

22 What's got six legs and can fly long distances?
Three swallows.

23 What gets bigger and bigger as you take more away from it?
A hole.

24 What's the difference between a nightwatchman and a butcher?
One stays awake and the other weighs a steak.

25 What do you put in a barrel to make it lighter?
A hole.

26 What was the highest mountain before Mt Everest was discovered?
Mt Everest.

27 What is H_2O_4?
Drinking.

28 How many apples can you put in an empty box?
One. After that it's not empty anymore.

29 What has teeth but cannot eat?
A comb.

30 What side of an apple is the left side?
The side that hasn't been eaten.

31 What jam can't you eat?
A traffic jam.

32 What's black and white and eats like a horse?
A zebra.

33 What are two things you cannot have for breakfast?
Lunch and dinner.

34 What's the difference between a young lady and a fresh loaf?
One is a well-bred maid and the other is well-made bread.

35 On what nuts can pictures hang?
Walnuts.

36 Why did the Invisible Man's wife understand him so well?
Because she could see right through him.

37 If you have a referee in football, what do you have in bowls?
Cornflakes.

38 Which cheese is made backwards?
Edam.

39 What vegetable goes well with jacket potatoes?
Button mushrooms.

40 How do you make a banana split?
Cut it in half.

41 What can you serve, but never eat?
A tennis ball.

42 When will water stop flowing downhill?
When it reaches the bottom.

43 What kind of cup can't hold water?
A cupcake.

44 What is round and deep but could not be filled up by all the water in the world?
A colander.

45 Three men were in a boat. It capsized but only two got their hair wet. Why?
The third man was bald.

46 What runs across the floor without legs?
Water.

47 What goes through water but doesn't get wet?
A ray of light.

48 What can't walk but can run?
A river.

49 What has holes and holds water?
A sponge.

50 What do you get if you jump into the Red Sea?
Wet.

51 What do you call a man who stands around and makes faces all day?
A clockmaker.

52 What has two hands, no fingers, stands still and goes?
A clock.

53 What is always behind the times?
The back of a watch.

54 Where does Friday come before Wednesday?
In the dictionary.

55 How many seconds are there in a year?
Twelve: 2nd of January, 2nd of February . . .

56 What did the burglar say to the lady who caught him stealing her silver?
'I'm at your service, ma'am.'

57 What did the buffalo say to his son, when he went away on a long trip?
'Bison.'

58 Why was number 10 scared?
Because 7 8 9 (seven ate nine).

59 What did one angel say to the other angel?
'Halo.'

60 What is always coming but never arrives?
Tomorrow.

61 Can February March?
No. But April May.

62 Which months have 28 days?
All of them.

63 Why can't it rain for two days in a row?
Because there is a night in between.

64 What is the beginning of eternity, the end of time, the beginning of every ending?
The letter 'e'.

65 Why did the girl tear the calendar?
Because she wanted to take a month off.

66 What's easier to give than receive?
Criticism.

67 What belongs to you but is used more by other people?
Your name.

68 What can you give away but also keep?
A cold.

69 What breaks when you say it?
Silence.

70 What's the definition of intense?
That's where campers sleep.

71 What did the shoe say to the foot?
'You're having me on.'

72 What's taken before you get it?
Your picture.

73 What's easy to get into but hard to get out of?
Trouble.

74 What kind of ship never sinks?
Friendship.

75 Why are good intentions like people who faint?
They need carrying out.

76 If a woman is born in China, grows up in Australia, goes to live in America and dies in New Orleans, what is she?
Dead.

77 Who swings through the cakeshop, yodelling?
Tarzipan.

78 What does every winner lose in a race?
Their breath.

79 What goes all around a pasture but never moves?
A fence.

80 What runs but doesn't get anywhere?
A refrigerator.

81 What flies around all day but never goes anywhere?
A flag.

82 Why is a ladies' belt like a garbage truck?
Because it goes around and around, and gathers the waist.

83 What ten-letter word starts with fuel?
A-U-T-O-M-O-B-I-L-E.

84 What stays in the corner and travels all around the world?
A postage stamp.

85 What can you hold but never touch?
A conversation.

86 What goes up and down but never moves?
A flight of stairs.

87 What goes up the chimney down, but not down the chimney up?
An umbrella.

88 What goes around the house and in the house but never touches the house?
The sun.

89 What goes up and does not come down?
Your age.

90 What question can you never answer yes to?
Are you asleep?

91 What starts working only when it's fired?
A rocket.

92 What's black when clean and white when dirty?
A blackboard.

93 What's green, has eight legs and would kill you if it fell on you from out of a tree?
A billiard table.

94 Why are false teeth like stars?
They come out at night.

95 What is the longest word in the world?
Smiles, because there is a mile between the beginning and the end.

96 What did the egg say to the whisk?
'I know when I'm beaten.'

97 What do you get if you cross a cowboy with a stew?
Hopalong casserole.

98 How does a boat show its affection?
By hugging the shore.

99 How does a fireplace feel?
Grate!

100 What do you draw without a pencil or paper?
A window shade.

101 Which room has no door, no windows, no floor and no roof?
A mushroom.

102 What is higher without the head than with it?
A pillow.

103 What sort of ring is always square?
A boxing ring!

104 What has a bottom at the top?
A leg.

105 The more you take, the more you leave behind. What am I?
Footsteps.

106 What has four legs and doesn't walk?
A table.

107 What has many rings but no fingers?
A telephone.

108 How long should a person's legs be?
Long enough to reach their feet.

109 Where can you always find a helping hand?
At the end of your arm.

110 How do you make a hot dog stand?
Steal its chair.

111 What did the stamp say to the envelope?
'Stick with me and we will go places.'

112 What has a hundred limbs but cannot walk?
A tree.

113 What do hippies do?
They hold your leggies on.

114 What's another word for tears?
Glumdrops.

115 What did one wall say to the other wall?
'I'll meet you at the corner.'

116 What's the last thing you take off before bed?
Your feet off the floor.

117 What do you call someone who doesn't have all their fingers on one hand?
Normal. You have fingers on both hands.

118 I have ten legs, 20 arms and 54 feet. What am I?
A liar.

119 What has no legs but can walk?
A pair of shoes.

120 What has four fingers and a thumb but is not a hand?
A glove!

121 How do you get four suits for a couple of dollars?
Buy a pack of cards.

122 What has a hundred legs but can't walk?
Fifty pairs of pants.

123 What bow can't be tied?
A rainbow.

124 When is a chair like a woman's dress?
When it's satin.

125 What did the tie say to the hat?
'You go on ahead, I'll just hang around.'

126 Who is scared of wolves and swears?
Little Rude Riding Hood.

127 What did the pencil sharpener say to the pencil?
'Stop going in circles and get to the point!'

128 Where do you find giant snails?
At the ends of their fingers.

129 What kind of dress can never be worn?
Your address.

130 What does a girl look for, but hopes she'll never find?
A hole in her pantyhose.

131 What's the difference between an oak tree and a tight shoe?
One makes acorns, the other makes corns ache.

132 How do you make a pair of trousers last?
Make the coat first.

133 What kind of coat can you put on only when it's wet?
A coat of paint.

134 What is at the end of the world?
The letter 'd'.

135 What are the four letters the dentist says when a patient visits him?
ICDK (I see decay).

136 What starts with a 'p', ends with an 'e', and has a million letters in it?
Post office.

137 What's the centre of gravity?
The letter 'v'.

138 What's the hottest letter in the alphabet?
It's 'b', because it makes oil boil!

139 Why is an island like the letter 't'?
Because it's in the middle of water.

140 How do you saw the sea in half?
With a sea-saw.

141 Why did the traffic light turn red?
You would too if you had to change in the middle of the street!

142 What starts with an 'e', ends with an 'e', and only has one letter in it?
An envelope!

143 What's the letter that ends everything?
The letter 'g'.

144 When does the alphabet only have 24 letters?
When U and I aren't there.

145 How do you spell 'mouse trap' with three letters?
C A T.

146 Why are old dinosaur bones kept in a museum?
Because they can't find any new ones.

147 What did the little mountain say to the big mountain?
'Hi Cliff!'

148 When Adam introduced himself to Eve, what three words did he use which read the same, backward and forward?
'Madam, I'm Adam.'

149 Who gets the sack every time he goes to work?
The postman.

150 How can you tell an undertaker?
By his grave manner.

151 What is the difference between a jeweller and a jailer?
A jeweller sells watches and a jailer watches cells.

152 Why can't anyone stay angry with actors?
Because they always make up.

153 What did one raindrop say to the other?
'Two's company, three's a cloud.'

154 What do you call a man who shaves 15 times a day?
A barber.

155 Why did the boy laugh after his operation?
Because the doctor put him in stitches.

156 Why didn't the boy go to work in the wool factory?
Because he was too young to dye.

157 Where do you find baby soldiers?
In the infantry.

158 When do mathematicians die?
When their number is up.

159 Which of the witch's friends eats the fastest?
The goblin.

160 What would you call superman if he lost all his powers?
Man.

161 Name three inventions that have helped man up in the world.
The elevator, the ladder and the alarm clock.

162 How did the Vikings send messages?
By Norse code.

163 What was more useful than the invention of the first telephone?
The second telephone.

164 When is the cheapest time to phone friends?
When they're not home.

165 If nothing ever sticks to Teflon, how does Teflon stick to the pan?

166 What was the best thing before sliced bread?

167 Why did the balloon burst?
Because it saw a lolly pop.

168 Why did the farmer plough his field with a steamroller?
He wanted to grow mashed potatoes.

169 What's the difference between an elephant and a matterbaby?
'What's a matterbaby?'
Nothing, but thanks for asking!

170 What did the big hand of the clock say to the little hand?
'Got a minute?'

171 When is a door not a door?
When it is ajar.

172 What has four wheels and flies?
A garbage truck.

173 Can a match box?
No, but a tin can.

174 When is a car like a frog?
When it is being toad.

175 What do all the Smiths in the phone book have in common?
They all have phones.

176 If a horse loses its tail, where could it get another?
At a re-tail store.

177 How many animals did Moses fit in the Ark?
None, it was Noah's Ark.

178 How do you get down from an elephant?
You don't get down from an elephant, you get down from a duck.

179 What's bright orange and sounds like a parrot?
A carrot.

180 What does an octopus wear when it's cold?
A coat of arms.

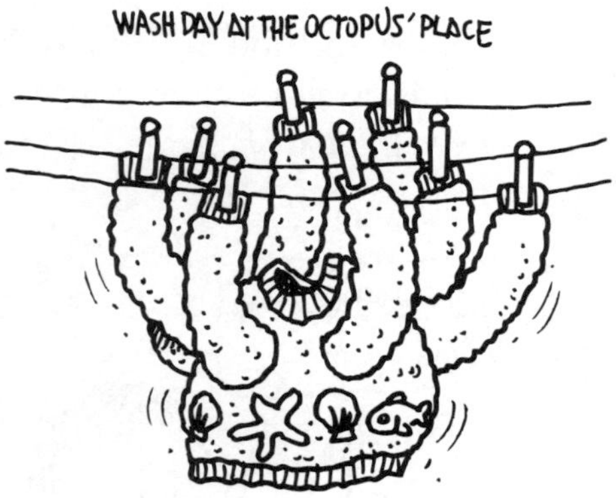

181 What's the difference between a dark sky and an injured lion?
One pours with rain, the other roars with pain.

182 What would you get if you crossed a hunting dog with a journalist?
A news hound.

183 If horses wear shoes what do camels wear?
Desert boots.

184 What do bees do with their honey?
They cell it.

185 How do you know when it's raining cats and dogs?
You step into a poodle.

186 What happened to two frogs that caught the same bug at the same time?
They got tongue-tied.

187 What can go as fast as a race horse?
The jockey!

188 Which bird never grows up?
The minor bird.

189 What do you call a cat who lives in a hospital?
A first aid kit.

190 Why is the letter 't' important to a stick insect?
Because without it, it would be a sick insect.

191 Why should you be careful when playing against a team of big cats?
They might be cheetahs.

192 What's the difference between a bird and a fly?
A bird can fly but a fly can't bird.

193 What kind of music does your father like to sing?
Pop music.

194 What did the parents say to their son who wanted to play drums?
'Beat it!'

195 What did the key say to the glue?
'You wanna be in show biz kid? Stick to me, I can open up doors for you!'

196 Where are the Andes?
At the end of your armies.

197 Why are dolphins clever?
Because they live in schools.

198 What is more fantastic than a talking dog?
A spelling bee!

199 When is a brown dog not a brown dog?
When it's a greyhound.

200 What is a prickly pear?
Two hedgehogs.

201 When is it bad luck to be followed by a big black cat?
When you are a little grey mouse.

202 Why does a tiger have stripes?
So it won't be spotted.

203 What flowers grow under your nose?
Tulips.

204 Which trees are always sad?
Pine trees.

205 What sort of star is dangerous?
A shooting star.

206 Why does lightning shock people?
It doesn't know how to conduct itself.

207 How do you make a fire with two sticks?
Make sure one of them is a match.

208 What did the didgeridoo?
Answered the phone when the boomerang.

209 How can you tell a dogwood tree?
By its bark.

210 What do you call a snowman with a suntan?
A puddle.

211 What kind of sharks never eat women?
Man-eating sharks!

212 What do you get if you cross the Atlantic with the Titanic?
About halfway.

213 Why are rivers lazy?
Because they never get off their beds.

214 What did the first mind reader say to the second mind reader?
'You're all right, how am I?'

215 Why does the ocean roar?
You would too if you had crabs on your bottom.

216 What trees do fortune tellers look at?
Palms.

217 Which goalkeeper can jump higher than a crossbar?
All of them – a crossbar can't jump!

218 What part of a football ground smells the best?
The scenter spot!

219 When is a baby like a basketball player?
When he dribbles.

220 Why did the footballer take a piece of rope onto the pitch?
He was the skipper!

221 What do you call a cat that plays football?
Puss in boots.

222 What illness do martial artists get?
Kung flu.

223 Why were the arrows nervous?
Because they were all in a quiver.

224 What has 22 legs and two wings but can't fly?
A soccer team.

225 What race is never run?
A swimming race.

226 Why did all the bowling pins go down?
Because they were on strike.

227 What's the best way to win a race?
Run faster than everyone else.

228 What washes up on very small beaches?
Microwaves.

229 What did the Pacific Ocean say to the Atlantic Ocean?
Nothing. It just waved.

230 What is big, red and eats rocks?
A big red rock eater.

231 What did the piece of wood say to the drill?
You bore me.

232 What do you call a boomerang that doesn't come back to you?
A stick.

233 What did one ear say to the other ear?
'Between you and me we need a haircut.'

234 What did the ear 'ear?
Only the nose knows.

235 Why was the glow-worm unhappy?
Her children weren't very bright.

236 Why are giraffes good friends to have?
Because they stick their necks out for you.

237 What do you get if you cross a worm with a baby goat?
A dirty kid.

238 What do you get when you cross an orange with a squash court?
Orange squash.

239 Why did the car get a puncture?
There was a fork in the road.

240 Why was the boxer known as Picasso?
Because he spent all his time on the canvas.

241 Why was the computer so tired when it got home?
Because it had a hard drive.

242 Why did the computer sneeze?
It had a virus.

243 What is a computer's first sign of old age?
Loss of memory.

244 Where do you find a no-legged dog?
Right where you left it.

245 What is the difference between a bus driver and a cold?
One knows the stops, the other stops the nose.

246 What fly has laryngitis?
A horsefly (hoarse fly).

247 What time do most people go to the dentist?
Tooth-hurty.

248 What illness do retired pilots get?
Flu.

249 When do clocks die?
When their time's up.

250 What is the only true cure for dandruff?
Baldness!

251 What's green and short and goes camping?
A boy sprout.

252 What happened when there was a fight in the fish and chip shop?
Two fish got battered.

253 What happened to the horse that swallowed a dollar coin?
He bucked.

254 What did the dentist say to the golfer?
'You've got a hole in one!'

255 What's the easiest way to find a pin in your carpet?
Walk around in your bare feet.

256 How did the comedian pass the time in hospital?
By telling sick jokes.

257 What do you call a ship that lies on the bottom of the ocean and shakes?
A nervous wreck.

258 What did the big chimney say to the little chimney?
'You're too young to smoke.'

259 What did the big telephone say to the little telephone?
'You're too young to be engaged.'

260 During which battle was Lord Nelson killed?
His last one.

261 What did Cinderella say when her photos didn't arrive?
'Some day my prints will come.'

262 Who delivers Christmas presents to the wrong houses?
Santa Flaws.

263 What did Santa Claus's wife say during a thunderstorm?
'Come and look at the rain, dear.'

264 Who was the father of the Black Prince?
Old King Coal.

265 Who was the fastest runner in the whole world?
Adam, because he was the first in the human race.

266 What do Alexander the Great and Kermit the Frog have in common?
The same middle name!

267 Where was Solomon's temple?
On his head.

268 Why was Thomas Edison able to invent the light bulb?
Because he was very bright.

269 What's the difference between Santa Claus and a warm dog?
Santa wears the suit, but a dog just pants.

270 Why did Henry VIII have so many wives?
He liked to chop and change.

271 Who steals from her grandma's house?
Little Red Robin Hood.

272 What did one tomato say to the other that was lagging behind? *'Ketchup!'*

273 Why don't bananas get lonely? *Because they hang around in bunches.*

274 Did Adam and Eve have a date? *No, they had an apple.*

275 When does 'b' come after 'u'? *When you take some of its honey.*

276 What kind of star wears sunglasses? *A movie star.*

277 How do you make a potato puff? *Chase it around the garden.*

278 What do you get when you cross a baby rabbit with a vegetable? *A bunion.*

279 What's small, round, white and giggles? *A tickled onion.*

280 What do you call two rows of vegetables? *A dual cabbageway.*

281 Why do watermelons get married? *Because they can't-elope.*

282 What's green, covered in custard and sad? *Apple grumble.*

283 Where were potatoes first found? *In the ground.*

284 If everyone bought a white car, what would we have? *A white carnation.*

285 Why is a bride always out of luck on her wedding day?
Because she never marries the best man.

286 Why did the snowman dress up?
Because he was going to the snowball.

287 If olive oil is made from olives and peanut oil is made from peanuts, what is baby oil made from?

288 What is a forum?
One-um plus three-um.

289 What is the smelliest sport?
Ping pong!

290 Why aren't football stadiums built in outer space?
Because there is no atmosphere!

291 What weapon was most feared by medieval knights?
A can opener.

292 Why do artists make lots of money?
Because they can draw their own wages.

293 What dance do hippies hate?
A square dance.

294 What did the ground say to the rain?
'If this keeps up, I'll be mud.'

295 How did Noah steer the Ark at night?
He switched on the floodlights.

296 Where are English kings and queens crowned?
On the head.

297 Why don't grasshoppers go to football matches?
They prefer cricket matches.

298 What's the easiest way to get on TV?
Sit on it.

299 Why is tennis such a noisy game?
Because everyone raises a racket.

300 What do you call a bee that is always complaining?
A grumble bee!

301 Why was the mother flea so sad?
Because her children were going to the dogs.

302 Where do old bowling balls end up?
In the gutter.

303 What is the difference between a hungry person and a greedy person?
One longs to eat, and the other eats too long.

304 Who is the smelliest person in the world?
King Pong.

305 What puzzles make you angry?
Crossword puzzles.

306 What's black and white and rolls down a hill?
A penguin.

307 What's black and white and laughs?
The penguin who pushed the other one.

308 Why was the maths book sad?
Because it had too many problems.

309 What happened when the bell fell into the swimming pool?
It got wringing wet.

310 Did you hear about the criminal contortionist?
He turned himself in.

311 What goes in pink and comes out blue?
A swimmer on a cold day!

312 Why did the belt go to jail?
Because it held up a pair of pants.

313 Why was the baby pen crying?
Because its mum was doing a long sentence.

314 What do you call a lazy toy?
An inaction figure.

315 Why did the bungy jumper take a vacation?
Because he was at the end of his rope.

316 What did the computer say to the programmer at lunchtime?
'Can I have a byte?'

317 What's the definition of minimum?
A very small mother.

318 Why was the broom late?
It overswept.

319 What are government workers called in Spain?
Seville servants.

320 Why do you go to bed?
Because the bed will not come to you.

321 Which bus could sail the oceans? *Columbus.*

322 How do fishermen make nets?
They make lots of holes and tie them together with string.

323 If a 7-Eleven is open 24 hours a day, 365 days a year, why are there locks on the doors?

324 What did the waterfall say to the fountain?
'You're just a little squirt.'

325 What did the dentist want?
The tooth, the whole tooth and nothing but the tooth.

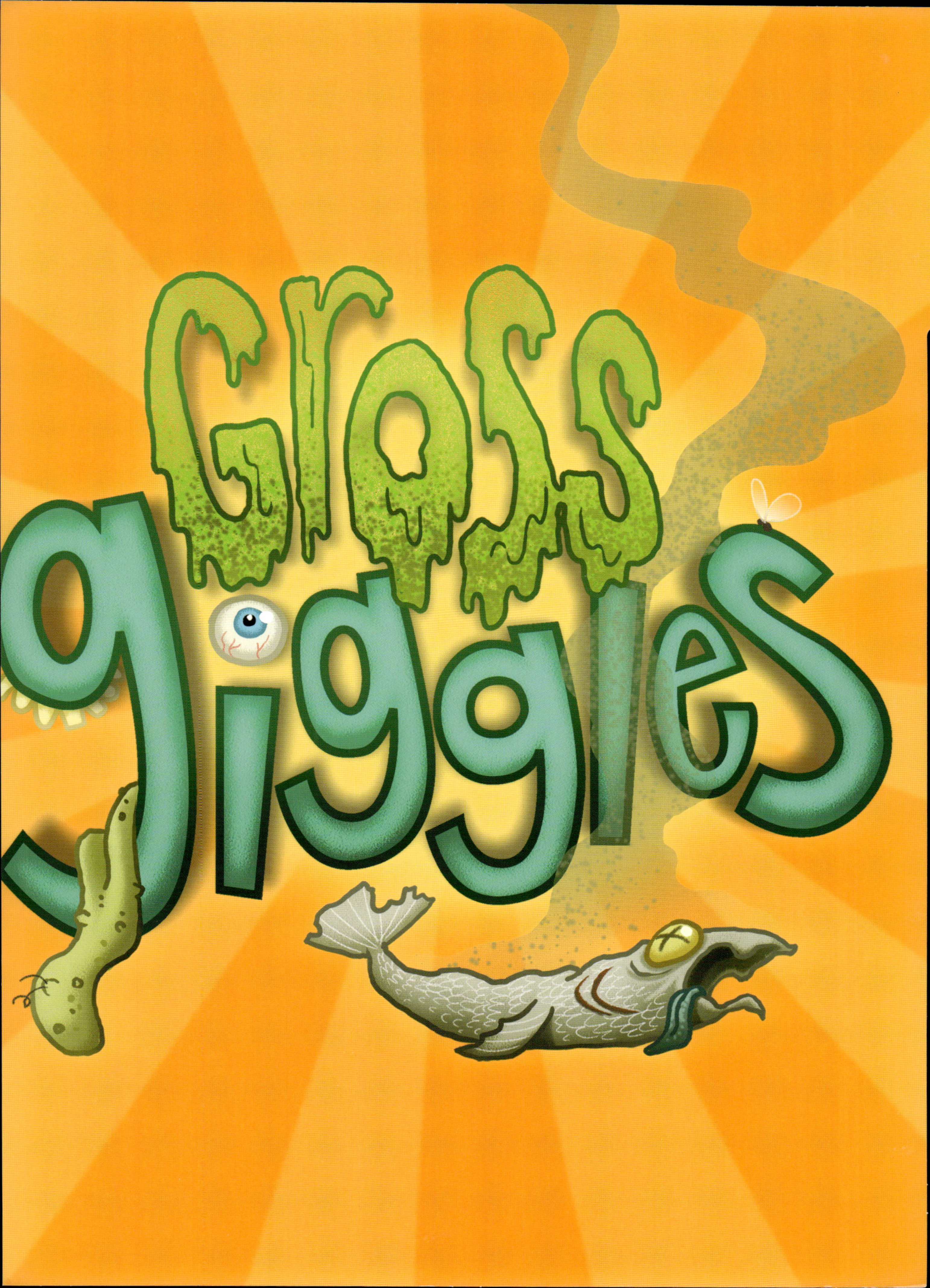
Gross Giggles

1 Did you hear the joke about the fart?
It stinks.

2 What's invisible and smells like carrots?
Bunny farts!

3 How can you tell when a moth farts?
He flies straight for a second.

4 What do you call an elephant that never washes?
A smellyphant.

5 What do you give an elephant with diarrhoea?
Plenty of room.

6 Doctor, Doctor, my husband smells like a fish.
Poor sole!

7 What has two grey legs and two brown legs?
An elephant with diarrhoea.

8 What makes you seasick?
Your little brother's vomit.

9 What do you give a sick elephant?
A very big paper bag.

10 What's yellow and smells of bananas?
Monkey vomit.

11 *'Your finger is in my soup bowl!'* said the man.
'Don't worry,' said the foolish waiter. *'The soup isn't hot.'*

12 What's a sick joke?
Something that comes up in conversation.

13 What's green, sticky and smells like eucalyptus?
Koala vomit.

14 Waiter, there's a fly in my soup.
Yes sir, the hot water killed it.

15 Waiter, what is this fly doing in my soup?
It looks like the backstroke.

16 Waiter, there's a fly in my soup.
Would you prefer him with your main course?

17 Waiter, there's a fly in my soup!
Don't worry sir, the spider in your salad will get it!

18 Waiter, there's a dead fly swimming in my soup.
That can't be, sir. Dead flies can't swim.

19 Waiter, are there snails on the menu?
Oh yes, sir, they must have escaped from the kitchen.

20 Waiter, there's a fly on my steak.
That's because it's attracted to rotting meat.

21 Waiter, there's a cockroach in my soup.
Sorry sir, we're all out of flies.

22 Waiter, there's a spider in my soup.
It must have eaten the fly.

23 Waiter, there's a fly in my soup.
No sir, that's a cockroach. The fly is on your roll.

24 Waiter, Waiter. There's a slug in my dinner.
Don't worry, sir, there's no extra charge.

25 Waiter, Waiter. There's a slug in my salad.
I'm sorry, sir, I didn't know you were a vegetarian.

26 Waiter, this egg is bad.
Well don't blame me, I only laid the table.

27 Waiter, please remove this fly.
But he hasn't finished yet.

28 Waiter, how did this fly get in my soup?
I guess it flew.

29 Waiter, what's this in my soup?
I don't know, sir. All bugs look the same to me.

30 Waiter, do you have frog legs?
Yes sir.
Then hop to the kitchen, and fetch me a steak.

31 Waiter, Waiter. There's a frog in my soup.
Don't worry, madam, there's not enough there to drown him.

32 Waiter, is there any soup on the menu?
No madam, I've wiped it all off.

33 Waiter, there's a bug in my soup.
Be quiet, sir, or everyone will want one.

34 Waiter, Waiter. There's a slug in my lettuce.
Sorry, Madam, no pets allowed here.

35 Waiter, bring me something to eat and make it snappy.
How about an alligator sandwich, sir?

36 Waiter, this soup tastes funny.
Why aren't you laughing then?

37 'Waiter, there is a small insect in my soup!
Sorry sir, I'll get you a bigger one!

38 Waiter, do you have frog legs?
No, I've always walked like this.

39 Waiter, Waiter. There are two worms on my plate.
Those are your sausages, sir.

40 Waiter, this crab only has one claw.
It must have been in a fight.
Then bring me the winner.

41 Waiter, what kind of soup is this?
Bean soup.
I don't care what it's been. What is it now?

42 Waiter, I'll have the soup and fish please.
I would recommend you eat the fish first. It's been sitting around for a few days and is beginning to smell.

43 Waiter, there's a fly in my soup.
That's because it's fly soup.

44 Waiter, there's a fly in my soup.
That's because the chef used to be a tailor.

45 Waiter, is this beef or lamb?
Can't you taste the difference?
No.
Then it doesn't matter.

46 Waiter, I'll have the burger please.
With pleasure.
No, with fries.

47 Waiter, we'll have two coffees please. And I want a clean cup.
Yes, sir. Here are your two coffees. Now which one of you wanted the clean cup?

48 Waiter, I'll have the lamb chops. And make them lean.
Certainly sir. To the right or the left?

49 Waiter, you have your thumb on my steak!
Well I didn't want to drop it again.

50 Waiter, how long will my hot dogs be?
Oh, about 20 centimetres.

51 Waiter, this apple pie is squashed.
Well you told me to step on it because you were in a hurry.

52 Waiter, I'm in a hurry. Will my pizza be long?
No, it will be round.

53 Waiter, I can't eat this meal. Please get the manager.
It's no use. He won't eat it either.

54 Waiter, this coffee tastes like mud.
I can't understand why. It was ground just a minute ago.

55 The cruise ship passenger was feeling really seasick, when the waiter asked if she'd like some lunch.
'No thanks', she replied. 'Just throw it over the side and save me the trouble.'

56 Two cannibals were having lunch.
'Are you almost finished?' said one to the other.
'Yes!' said the first. *'I'm on my last leg now!'*

57 What did the cannibal say to the explorer?
'Nice to eat you.'

58 What do you get if you cross a skunk with a bear?
Winnie the Poo.

59 What swings through the trees and is very dangerous?
A chimpanzee with a machine gun.

60 Waiter, there's a fly in my soup.
I find that hard to believe, sir. The chef used them all in the casserole.

61 What's the hardest part about skydiving?
The ground!

62 Why didn't the man die when he drank poison?
Because he was in the living room.

63 How do you make a Venetian blind?
Poke his eyes out.

64 What's green and slimy and hangs from trees?
Giraffe boogie.

65 What's Mozart up to now?
Decomposing.

66 What's green, sits in the corner and cries?
The Incredible Sulk.

67 Why don't elephants pick their noses?
Because they don't know what to do with 20-kilogram boogers.

68 Why do gorillas have big nostrils?
Because they have big fingers.

69 What do you find up a clean nose?
Fingerprints.

70 Doctor, Doctor, how can I stop my nose from running?
Stick your foot out and trip it.

71 What do you do if your nose goes on strike?
Picket.

72 How did the basketball court get wet?
The players dribbled all over it.

73 What did the dragon say when he saw the knight in his shining armour?
Oh no! Not more canned food.

74 What's green, has two legs, and sits on the end of your finger?
The boogeyman.

75 What's another name for a snail?
A booger with a crash helmet.

76 What is the difference between broccoli and boogers?
Kids don't like to eat broccoli!

77 What's green and slimy, and hangs from trees?
Giraffe boogers.

78 How do you make a tissue dance?
Put some boogie into it.

79 What's brown and sounds like a bell?
Dung.

80 What's tall, hairy, lives in the Himalayas and does 500 sit-ups a day?
The abdominal snowman.

81 Three girls walked into a beauty salon. Two had blonde hair and one had green hair. The hairdresser asked the blondes, *'Did you dye your hair blonde?'* *'Oh, it's natural,'* they replied. The hairdresser asked the other girl, *'Did you dye your hair green?'* She replied, *'Oh, it's natural. I put my hand on my nose and rubbed it into my hair.'*

82 What did one toilet say to the other toilet?
You look a bit flushed!

83 What did the first mate see in the toilet?
The captain's log.

84 Why did the surfer stop surfing?
Because the sea weed.

85 Why do petrol stations always lock their toilets?
They are afraid someone might clean them.

86 Someone stole all the toilet seats from the police station. The officers have nothing to go on.

87 Why did the boy take his own toilet paper to the birthday party?
Because he was a party pooper.

88 Why did the toilet paper roll down the hill?
To get to the bottom.

89 Why did Piglet look in the toilet?
He was looking for Pooh.

90 Where do dinosaurs go to the toilet?
In the dino-sewer.

91 Doctor, Doctor, I feel like an apple.
Well don't worry, I won't bite.

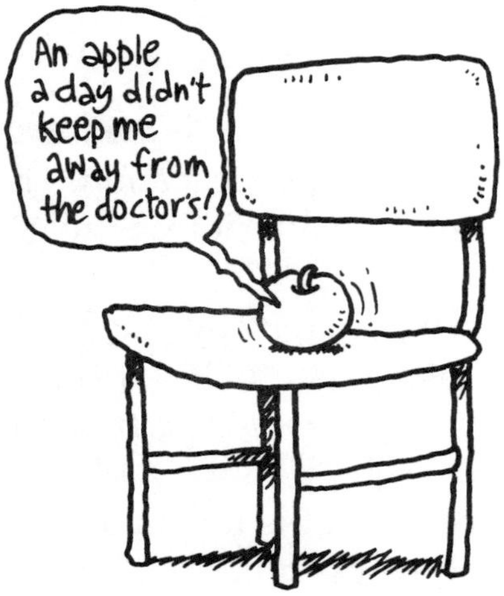

92 Doctor, Doctor, I swallowed a spoon.
Well try to relax and don't stir.

93 Doctor, Doctor, I feel like a strawberry.
I can see you're in a bit of a jam.

94 Doctor, Doctor, I dreamed that I ate a large marshmallow!
Did you wake up without a pillow?

95 Doctor, Doctor, I have a pain in the eye every time I drink hot chocolate!
Take the spoon out of your mug before you drink.

96 Doctor, Doctor, sometimes I feel like an onion, and sometimes I feel like a cucumber.
Boy, you're in a pickle.

97 Doctor, Doctor, what's wrong with me?
Well, you have a carrot up your nose, a bean in one ear, and a French fry in the other. I'd say you're not eating right.

98 Doctor, Doctor, I keep thinking I'm a fruitcake.
What's got into you?
Flour, raisins and cherries.

99 Doctor, Doctor, I'm turning into a wastebasket.
Don't give me a bunch of garbage.

100 Doctor, Doctor, I ate some oysters and now I'm feeling sick.
Were they fresh?
How can you tell?
You open the shell and look.
You're not supposed to eat the shell?

101 Doctor, Doctor, I have jelly in my ear.
You're just a trifle deaf.

102 Doctor, Doctor, the first thirty minutes I'm up every morning I feel dizzy. What should I do?
Get up half an hour later.

103 Doctor, Doctor, I feel like a pair of socks.
Well, I'll be darned.

104 Doctor, Doctor, I have yellow teeth. What should I do?
Wear a brown tie.

105 Doctor, Doctor, what's good for biting fingernails?
Very sharp teeth.

106 Doctor, Doctor, I've just swallowed a pen.
Well, sit down and fill out this form!

107 Doctor, Doctor, my eyesight is getting worse.
You're absolutely right, this is a post office.

108 Doctor, Doctor, I'm afraid of the dark.
Then leave the light on.

109 Doctor, Doctor, I keep stealing things.
Take one of these pills and if that doesn't work, bring me a computer.

110 Doctor, Doctor, this ointment you gave me makes my arm smart!
Try putting some on your head.

111 Doctor, Doctor, should I file my nails?
No, throw them away like everyone else does.

112 Doctor, Doctor, will this ointment clear up my spots?
I never make rash promises!

113 Doctor, Doctor, my leg hurts. What can I do?
Limp.

114 Doctor, Doctor, I can't feel my legs.
That's because we had to amputate your arms.

115 Doctor, Doctor, I snore so loud, I wake myself up!
Try sleeping in another room.

116 Doctor, Doctor, sometimes I feel like a goat.
How long has this been going on?
Ever since I was a kid.

117 Doctor, Doctor, I think I'm a snail.
Don't worry, we'll have you out of your shell soon.

118 Doctor, Doctor, I think I'm an adder.
Great, can you help me with my accounts please?

119 Doctor, Doctor, I think I'm an electric eel.
That's shocking!

120 Doctor, Doctor, my sister thinks she's a squirrel.
Sounds like a nut case to me.

121 Doctor, Doctor, I feel like a sheep.
That's baaaaaaaaad!

122 Doctor, Doctor, I think I'm a mouse trap!
Well, snap out of it.

123 Doctor, Doctor, I feel like a racehorse.
Take one of these every four laps!

124 Doctor, Doctor, I keep thinking I'm a spider.
What a web of lies!

125 Doctor, Doctor, I feel like a toad.
Don't worry! We have hoperations for that these days.

126 Doctor, Doctor, my wife thinks she's a chicken.
Do you want me to cure her?
No, I just wondered if you wanted some eggs.

127 Doctor, Doctor, I think I'm a bridge.
What's come over you?
Oh, two cars, a large truck and a bus.

128 Doctor, Doctor, I keep thinking I'm a mosquito.
What a sucker!

129 Doctor, Doctor, I think I'm a moth.
Get out of the way, you're in my light!

130 Doctor, Doctor, I feel like a bird.
I'll tweet you in a minute.

131 Doctor, Doctor, I keep thinking I'm a bee.
Buzz off, I'm busy.

132 Doctor, Doctor, I think I'm a frog.
What's wrong with that?
I think I'm going to croak!

133 Doctor, Doctor, I think I'm a python.
You can't get around me like that, you know!

134 Doctor, Doctor, I keep thinking I'm a yoyo.
How are you feeling?
Oh, up and down.

135 Doctor, Doctor, people keep disagreeing with me.
No they don't.

136 Doctor, Doctor, I think I'm a woodworm.
How boring for you!

137 Doctor, Doctor, I think I'm a snake, about to shed my skin.
Why don't you go behind the screen and slip into something more comfortable!

138 Doctor, Doctor, my girlfriend thinks she's a duck.
You'd better bring her in to see me right away.
I can't – she's already flown south for the winter.

139 Doctor, Doctor, my pig has a rash. What should I do?
Try this oinkment.

140 Doctor, Doctor, I think I'm a nit.
Will you get out of my hair?

141 Doctor, Doctor, I keep seeing green aliens with two heads and four legs.
Have you seen a psychiatrist?
No, just green aliens with two heads and four legs.

142 Doctor, Doctor, I think I'm a rubber band.
Why don't you stretch yourself out on the couch there, and tell me all about it?

143 Doctor, Doctor, something is preying on my mind!
Don't worry, it will probably starve to death.

144 Doctor, Doctor, I keep thinking I'm a dog.
Well, get up on the couch and I'll examine you.
I can't, I'm not allowed on the furniture.

145 Doctor, Doctor, sometimes I think there are two of me.
Good, you can pay both bills on your way out.

146 Doctor, Doctor, I think I'm a clock.
You're winding me up.

147 Doctor, Doctor, I feel like a tennis racquet.
You must be too highly strung.

148 Doctor, Doctor, I think I'm turning into a woman.
Well, you are 16 now Amanda.

149 Doctor, Doctor, my wife thinks I'm crazy because I like hamburgers.
That's ridiculous. I like hamburgers too.
Good, you should come by and see my collection some time. I have hundreds of them.

150 Doctor, Doctor, my stomach hurts.
Stop your belly aching.

151 Doctor, Doctor, I feel like a bell.
Well, take these and if they don't work, give me a ring.

152 Doctor, Doctor, when I press with my finger here . . . it hurts, and here . . . it hurts, and here . . . and here! What do you think is wrong with me?
Your finger's broken.

153 Doctor, Doctor, do you have something for a migraine?
Take this hammer and hit yourself on the foot. You'll forget about your headache.

154 Doctor, Doctor, I keep thinking I'm a doorknob.
Well, don't fly off the handle.

155 Doctor, Doctor, can you give me anything for excessive wind?
Sure, here's a kite.

156 Doctor, Doctor, I have a terrible cough!
Then you should practise.

157 Doctor, Doctor, I tend to flush a lot.
Don't worry, it's just a chain reaction.

158 Doctor, Doctor, my wife keeps beating me.
Oh dear. How often?
Every time we play Scrabble.

159 Doctor, Doctor, my wife's contractions are only five minutes apart.
Is this her first child?
No, this is her husband.

160 Doctor, Doctor, these pills you gave me for body odour. . .
What's wrong with them?
They keep slipping out from under my arms!

161 Doctor, Doctor, I feel like a dog.
Then go see a vet!

162 Doctor, Doctor, you've taken out my tonsils, my appendix, my gall bladder and one of my kidneys, but I still feel sick.
That's enough out of you.

163 Doctor, Doctor, how much to have this splinter taken out?
Seventy dollars.
Seventy dollars for just a couple of minutes' work?
I can pull it out very slowly if you like.

164 Doctor, Doctor, tell me straight. Is it bad?
Just don't start watching any new TV series.

165 Doctor, Doctor, how was my check-up?
Perfect. You'll live to be 80.
But I am 80.
In that case, it's been nice knowing you.

166 Doctor, Doctor, can I have a bottle of aspirin and a pot of glue?
Why?
Because I have a splitting headache!

167 Doctor, Doctor, I'm at death's door.
Don't worry, I'll pull you through.

168 Doctor, Doctor, can you help me out?
Certainly – which way did you come in?

169 Doctor, Doctor, I came as quick as I could. What's the problem?
Your lab results are back and you only have 24 hours to live.
That's terrible.
There's worse news. I've been trying to call you since yesterday.

170 Doctor, Doctor, how long have I got?
Ten.
Ten what? Ten months? Ten weeks?
10, 9, 8, 7. . .

171 Doctor, Doctor, I only have 59 seconds to live!
Just a minute!

172 Doctor, Doctor, my son swallowed my razor blade.
Well, just use an electric razor.

173 Doctor, Doctor, everyone keeps throwing me in the garbage.
Don't talk rubbish!

174 Doctor, Doctor, my baby swallowed some explosives.
Well, keep calm. We don't want him to go off.

175 Doctor, Doctor, did you hear about the boy who swallowed a coin?
No? Well, there's no change yet!

176 Doctor, Doctor, I keep thinking there's two of me.
One at a time please!

177 Doctor, Doctor, I was playing a kazoo and I swallowed it.
Lucky you weren't playing the piano.

178 Doctor, Doctor, I can't get to sleep.
Sit on the edge of the bed and you'll drop off.

179 Doctor, Doctor, my hair is falling out. Can you give me something to keep it in?
Yes, a paper bag.

180 Doctor, Doctor, my belly is so big that I'm embarrassed by it. What can I do?
Have you tried to diet?
Yes, but the different colours do not seem to make a difference.

181 Doctor, Doctor, some days I feel like a teepee and other days I feel like a wigwam.
You're two tents!

182 Doctor, Doctor, I swallowed a bone.
Are you choking?
No, I really did!

183 What's the difference between school lunches and a pile of slugs?
School lunches are in lunch boxes.

184 How do you keep flies out of the kitchen?
Put a pile of manure in the living room.

185 How do you know your kitchen is filthy?
The slugs leave trails on the floor that read 'Clean me'.

186 What's the difference between a maggot and a cockroach?
Cockroaches crunch more when you eat them.

187 What do you get if you run a sparrow over with a lawn mower?
Shredded tweet.

188 Did you hear about the cannibal who gnawed a bone for hours on end?
When he stood up, he fell over.

189 What do you get if you cross an elephant with a box of laxatives?
Out of the way.

190 What's an army of worms called?
An apple corps.

191 Why do little brothers chew with their mouths full?
Flies have to live somewhere.

192 What's yellow, brown and hairy?
Cheese on toast dropped on the carpet.

193 What's worse than finding a worm in your apple?
Finding half a worm!

194 Mummy, Mummy, I can't find the dog's food.
Don't worry about it. Eat your stew.

195 Hey! There's no chicken in this chicken pot pie.
Well, do you expect to find dogs in dog biscuits?

196 What do you get if you sit under a cow?
A pat on the head.

197 Why did the lizard cross the road?
To see his flat mate.

198 Johnny, I think your dog likes me. He's been looking at me all night.
That's because you're eating out of his bowl.

199 What has four legs and flies?
A dead cat.

200 Boy: '*Dad, there's a black cat in the dining room!*'
Dad: '*That's okay, Son, black cats are lucky.*'
Son: '*This one is – he ate your dinner!*'

201 What's green and red and goes at 120 km/h?
A frog in a blender.

202 What's black and white and red all over?
A zebra in a blender.

203 Why are naughty kids like maggots?
Because they try to wriggle out of everything.

204 What's the last thing that goes through a bug's mind when he hits a car windscreen?
His bottom.

205 What has 50 legs and can't walk?
Half a centipede.

206 Why did the Cyclops give up teaching?
Because he only had one pupil.

207 Why are sausages so bad mannered?
They spit in the frying pan.

208 What do you call the red stuff between an elephant's toes?
A slow explorer.

209 Where does your nose go to eat?
Booger King.

210 How do you make antifreeze?
Lock her outside in the cold.

211 What did one maggot say to another?
What's a nice girl like you doing in a joint like this?

212 Why did the one-handed man cross the road?
He wanted to get to the secondhand shop!

213 What baseball position did the boy with no arms or legs play?
First base.

214 How did the rude woman cook dinner?
On a spit roast.

215 Why don't cannibals eat comedians?
Because they taste funny.

216 What is the soft stuff between sharks' teeth?
Slow swimmers.

217 What has four legs and an arm?
A happy lion.

218 Why did the shark take so long to eat a victim's arm?
Because the victim's watch made it time-consuming.

219 Person 1: *'Pssst. Do you want to buy the genuine skull of Julius Caesar?'*
Person 2: *'You sold me his skull last week. Besides, that one is smaller.'*
Person 1: *'This is when he was a boy.'*

220 How did the dentist become a brain surgeon?
His drill slipped.

221 What's old, wrinkled and puts away your underwear?
Your grandma.

222 Why did the bacteria cross the microscope?
To get to the other slide.

223 What do you get when you cross a rooster with a steer?
A cock and bull story.

224 When the fat man was run over by a steamroller, what was proved?
That he had a lot of guts.

225 What's brown and sounds like a bell?
Dung.

226 Mummy, Mummy, why can't we buy a garbage disposal?
You're doing a fine job chewing.

227 What do you call a lamb with a machine gun?
Lambo.

228 What's the difference between an oral thermometer and a rectal thermometer?
The taste.

229 What do you say when you meet a toad?
Wart's new?

230 Why do farts smell?
So that deaf people can appreciate them too.

231 What's the nearest thing to silver?
The Lone Ranger's bottom.

232 Did you hear about the two fat men who ran a marathon?
One ran in short bursts, the other ran in burst shorts.

233 What is 20 feet long and smells musty?
Line dancing at the old people's home.

234 Why are basketball players never asked for dinner?
Because they're always dribbling.

235 Three guys, Shut-up, Manners and Poop, drove too fast and Poop fell out of the car. Shut-up went to the police station, where the policeman asked, *'What's your name?'*
'Shut-up,' he answered.
'Hey – where are your manners!' the policeman exclaimed.
Shut-up replied, *'Outside on the road, scrapin' up Poop!'*

236 Mummy, I don't want to go to Europe.
Just keep swimming.

237 What happens when the Queen burps?
She issues a royal pardon.

238 Roger was in a full bus when an extremely large lady opposite said to him, *'If you were a gentleman, you'd stand up and let someone else sit down.'*
'And if you were a lady,' Roger replied, *'you'd stand up and let four people sit down!'*

239 Mummy, Mummy, can I lick the bowl?
No! You'll have to flush like everyone else.

240 Mummy, Mummy, Dad has been run over by a steamroller.
Just slide him under the door.

241 Mummy, Mummy, I have a splinter in my finger!
Scratching your head again?

242 What colour is a hiccup?
Burple.

243 What did the alien say to the plant?
'Take me to your weeder.'

244 What did the alien say to her son when he returned home?
'Where on Earth have you been?'

245 Who is big and hairy, wears a dress and climbs the Empire State Building?
Queen Kong.

246 What did King Kong say when his sister had a baby?
Well I'll be a monkey's uncle.

247 What do you get when an elephant stands on your roof?
Mushed rooms.

248 What did the alien say to the petrol pump?
Take your finger out of your ear when I'm talking to you.

249 Why did the executioner go to work early?
To get a head start.

250 What's green, sits in the corner and cries?
The Incredible Sulk.

251 What animal builds his house in the jungle?
A boa constructor.

252 What's brown and sticky?
A stick.

253 What did the floor say to the desk?
I can see your drawers.

254 How did the skunk phone his mother?
On a smellular phone.

255 Who is King of the Cannibals?
Henry the Ate.

256 What's the hardest part of making dinosaur stew?
Finding a pot big enough to hold the dinosaur.

257 What do you call a man with a spade?
Doug!

258 . . . a man without a spade?
Douglas!

259 . . . a woman with a cat on her head?
Kitty!

260 . . . a man with a large black and blue mark on his leg?
Bruce!

261 . . . a man with a seagull on his head?
Cliff!

262 . . . a man pouring water into a jug?
Phil!

263 . . . a man with a licence plate on his head?
Reg!

264 . . . a woman with a Christmas tree on her head?
Carol!

265 . . . a woman with one leg?
Eileen!

266 . . . a man with a Christmas tree on his head?
Noel!

267 . . . a woman with a toilet on her head?
Lu!

268 . . . a woman with two toilets on her head?
Lulu!

269 . . . a man with a kilt on his head?
Scott!

270 . . . a man with some cat scratches?
Claude!

271 . . . a man in a pile of leaves?
Russell!

272 . . . a lady standing in the middle of a tennis court?
Annette!

273 . . . a superhero that got run over by a steamroller?
Flatman!

274 . . . a woman with a tortoise on her head?
Shelley!

275 . . . a man floating in the sea?
Bob!

276 . . . a woman with a twig on her head?
Hazel!

277 . . . a man with a plank on his head?
Edward!

278 . . . a Russian gardener?
Ivanhoe!

279 . . . a girl with a frog on her head?
Lily!

280 . . . a woman with a breeze on her head?
Gail!

281 . . . a man with a legal document on his head?
Will!

282 . . . a girl with one foot on each side of a river?
Bridget!

283 . . . a woman who climbs up walls?
Ivy!

284 . . . a man who is always around when you need him?
Andy!

285 . . . a man with a stamp on his head?
Frank!

286 . . . a man with rabbits in his pants?
Warren!

287 When do you put a frog in your sister's bed?
When you can't find a mouse.

288 Why don't turkeys get invited to dinner parties?
Because they use fowl language.

289 What do frogs order in restaurants?
French Flies!

290 If you were making a large omelette, would you use chicken eggs or elephant eggs?
Chicken eggs! Elephant yolks are so bad.

291 What do you get if you pour hot water down a rabbit hole?
Hot cross bunnies.

292 Did you put the cat out?
I didn't know it was on fire.

293 What do you call a man with an elephant on his head?
Squashed.

294 What did the slug say as he slipped down the window very fast?
How slime flies.

295 Did you hear about the performer who specialised in bird impressions?
He ate worms.

296 What do polar bears get from sitting on the ice too long?
Polaroids.

297 What do worms leave round their bathtubs?
The scum of the earth.

Knock
Knock
Nonsense

1 **K**nock Knock. *Who's there?*
Ammonia! *Ammonia who?*
Ammonia little girl who can't reach the doorbell!

2 **K**nock Knock. *Who's there?*
Ahmed! *Ahmed who?*
Ahmed a mistake! I think I want the house next door!

3 **K**nock Knock. *Who's there?*
Venice! *Venice who?*
Venice your doorbell going to be fixed?

4 **K**nock Knock. *Who's there?*
Don! *Don who?*
Don just stand there! Open the door!

5 **K**nock Knock. *Who's there?*
Max! *Max who?*
Max no difference who it is – just open the door!

6 **K**nock Knock. *Who's there?*
Havalock! *Havalock who?*
Havalock put on your door!

7 **K**nock Knock. *Who's there?*
Avon! *Avon who?*
Avon you to open the door!

8 **K**nock Knock. *Who's there?*
Bolton! *Bolton who?*
Bolton the door! That's why I can't get in!

9 **K**nock Knock. *Who's there?*
Malcolm! *Malcolm who?*
Malcolm you won't open the door?

10 **K**nock Knock. *Who's there?*
Ben! *Ben who?*
Ben knocking on the door all afternoon!

11 **K**nock Knock. *Who's there?*
Ivor! *Ivor who?*
Ivor you let me in or I'll break the door down!

12 **K**nock Knock. *Who's there?*
Dish! *Dish who?*
Dish is getting boring! Open the door!

13 **K**nock Knock. *Who's there?*
Letter! *Letter who?*
Letter in or she'll knock the door down!

14 **K**nock Knock. *Who's there?*
Ferdie! *Ferdie who?*
Ferdie last time open the door!

15 **K**nock Knock. *Who's there?*
Aitch! *Aitch who?*
Do you need a tissue?

16 **K**nock Knock. *Who's there?*
Turnip! *Turnip who?*
Turnip the heater, it's cold in here!

17 **K**nock Knock. *Who's there?*
Ahab! *Ahab who?*
Ahab to go to the toilet now! Quick, open the door!

18 **K**nock Knock. *Who's there?*
Arch! *Arch who?*
Bless you!

19 **K**nock Knock. *Who's there?*
Aida! *Aida who?*
Aida whole box of cookies and now I feel sick!

20 **K**nock Knock. *Who's there?*
Lion! *Lion who?*
Lion down is the best thing to do when you're sick!

21 **K**nock Knock. *Who's there?*
Paine! *Paine who?*
Paine in my stomach! I need some medicine!

22 **K**nock Knock. *Who's there?*
Diesel! *Diesel who?*
Diesel help with your cold! Take two every four hours!

23 **K**nock Knock. *Who's there?*
Tish! *Tish who?*
Bless you!

24 **K**nock Knock. *Who's there?*
Artichokes! *Artichokes who?*
Artichokes when he eats too fast!

25 **K**nock Knock. *Who's there?*
Alf! *Alf who?*
Alf all if you don't catch me!

26 **K**nock Knock. *Who's there?*
Eiffel! *Eiffel who?*
Eiffel down!

27 **K**nock Knock. *Who's there?*
Carrie! *Carrie who?*
Carrie me inside, I'm exhausted!

28 **K**nock Knock. *Who's there?*
M-2! *M-2 who?*
M-2 tired to knock!

29 **K**nock Knock. *Who's there?*
Pinza! *Pinza who?*
Pinza needles!

30 **K**nock Knock. *Who's there?*
Gotter! *Gotter who?*
Gotter go to the toilet!

31 **K**nock Knock. *Who's there?*
Arncha! *Arncha who?*
Arncha going to let me in?
It's freezing out here!

32 **K**nock Knock. *Who's there?*
Claire! *Claire who?*
Claire the snow from your path
or someone will have an accident!

33 **K**nock Knock. *Who's there?*
Butter! *Butter who?*
Butter wear a coat when you
come out. It's cold!

34 **K**nock Knock. *Who's there?*
Lettuce! *Lettuce who?*
Lettuce in, it's cold outside!

35 **K**nock Knock. *Who's there?*
Scold! *Scold who?*
Scold out here, let me in!

36 **K**nock Knock. *Who's there?*
Bart! *Bart who?*
Bartween you and me, I'm sick
of standing in the cold!

37 **K**nock Knock. *Who's there?*
Alaska! *Alaska who?*
Alaska one more time.
Please let me in!

38 **K**nock Knock. *Who's there?*
Jilly! *Jilly who?*
Jilly out here, so let me in!

39 **K**nock Knock. *Who's there?*
Alaska! *Alaska who?*
Alaska no questions! You tella
no lies!

40 **K**nock Knock. *Who's there?*
Ice-cream! *Ice-cream who?*
Ice-cream, you scream!

41 **K**nock Knock. *Who's there?*
Freeze! *Freeze who?*
Freeze a jolly good fellow!

42 **K**nock Knock. *Who's there?*
Felix! *Felix who?*
Felix my ice-cream, I'll lick his!

43 **K**nock Knock. *Who's there?*
Icy! *Icy who?*
I see your underwear!

44 **K**nock Knock. *Who's there?*
Ice-cream soda! *Ice-cream soda who?*
Ice-cream soda neighbours
wake up!

45 **K**nock Knock. *Who's there?*
Snow. *Snow who?*
Snow good asking me!

46 **K**nock Knock. *Who's there?*
Gorilla! *Gorilla who?*
Gorilla cheese sandwich for me, please!

47 **K**nock Knock. *Who's there?*
Guinea! *Guinea who?*
Guinea some money so I can buy some food!

48 **K**nock Knock. *Who's there?*
Zubin! *Zubin who?*
Zubin eating garlic again!

49 **K**nock Knock. *Who's there?*
Brie! *Brie who?*
Brie me my supper!

50 **K**nock Knock. *Who's there?*
Hammond! *Hammond who?*
Hammond eggs for breakfast please!

51 **K**nock Knock. *Who's there?*
Bacon! *Bacon who?*
Bacon a cake for your birthday!

52 **K**nock Knock. *Who's there?*
Cash! *Cash who?*
Are you a nut?

53 **K**nock Knock. *Who's there?*
Curry! *Curry who?*
Curry me back home please!

54 **K**nock Knock. *Who's there?*
Cheese! *Cheese who?*
Cheese a jolly good fellow!

55 **K**nock Knock. *Who's there?*
Cantaloupe! *Cantaloupe who?*
Cantaloupe with you tonight!

56 **K**nock Knock. *Who's there?*
Crispin! *Crispin who?*
Crispin juicy is how I like my chicken!

57 **K**nock Knock. *Who's there?*
Chicken! *Chicken who?*
Chicken your pocket!
My keys might be there!

58 **K**nock Knock. *Who's there?*
The Sultan! *The Sultan who?*
The Sultan Pepper!

59 **K**nock Knock. *Who's there?*
Les! *Les who?*
Les go out for dinner!

60 **K**nock Knock. *Who's there?*
Mayonnaise! *Mayonnaise who?*
Mayonnaise are hurting!
I think I need glasses!

61 **K**nock Knock. *Who's there?*
Noah! *Noah who?*
Noah good place for a meal?

62 **K**nock Knock. *Who's there?*
Wafer! *Wafer who?*
Wafer a long time but
I'm back now!

63 **K**nock Knock. *Who's there?*
Phyllis! *Phyllis who?*
Phyllis a glass of water will you!

64 **K**nock Knock. *Who's there?*
Olive! *Olive who?*
Olive in that house across the road!

65 **K**nock Knock. *Who's there?*
P! *P who?*
P nuts, P nuts, get your fresh
P nuts!

66 **K**nock Knock. *Who's there?*
Olive! *Olive who?*
Olive you!

67 **K**nock Knock. *Who's there?*
Water! *Water who?*
Water friends for!

68 **K**nock Knock. *Who's there?*
Vitamin! *Vitamin who?*
Vitamin for a party!

69 **K**nock Knock. *Who's there?*
Pa! *Pa who?*
Pa-tridge in a pear tree!

70 **K**nock Knock. *Who's there?*
X! *X who?*
X for breakfast!

71 **K**nock Knock. *Who's there?*
Pear! *Pear who?*
Pear of freeloaders out here
wanting some dinner!

72 **K**nock Knock. *Who's there?*
Parsley! *Parsley who?*
Parsley mustard please!

73 **K**nock Knock. *Who's there?*
Pecan! *Pecan who?*
Pecan someone your own size!

74 **K**nock Knock. *Who's there?*
Gizza! *Gizza who?*
Gizza kiss!

75 **K**nock Knock. *Who's there?*
Arthur! *Arthur who?*
Arthur any more at home like you!

76 **K**nock Knock. *Who's there?*
Jimmy! *Jimmy who?*
Jimmy a little kiss on the cheek!

77 **K**nock Knock. *Who's there?*
Aardvark! *Aardvark who?*
Aardvark a million miles for one of your smiles!

78 **K**nock Knock. *Who's there?*
Harley! *Harley who?*
Harley ever see you any more!

79 **K**nock Knock. *Who's there?*
Army! *Army who?*
Army and you still friends?

80 **K**nock Knock. *Who's there?*
Adore! *Adore who?*
Adore is between us, open up!

81 **K**nock Knock. *Who's there?*
Adore! *Adore who?*
Adore is for knocking on!

82 **K**nock Knock. *Who's there?*
Avon! *Avon who?*
Avon you to be my wife!

83 **K**nock Knock. *Who's there?*
Ida! *Ida who?*
(sings) Ida know why I love you like I do!

84 **K**nock Knock. *Who's there?*
Harlow! *Harlow who?*
Harlow Dolly!

85 **K**nock Knock. *Who's there?*
Cecil! *Cecil who?*
Cecil have music wherever she goes!

86 **K**nock Knock. *Who's there?*
Larva! *Larva who?*
I larva you!

87 **K**nock Knock. *Who's there?*
Leonie! *Leonie who?*
Leonie one for me!

88 **K**nock Knock. *Who's there?*
Marie! *Marie who?*
Marie the one you love!

89 **K**nock Knock. *Who's there?*
Luke! *Luke who?*
Luke through the peephole and you'll see!

90 **K**nock Knock. *Who's there?*
Jean! *Jean who?*
Jean-ius! Ask me a question!

91 **K**nock Knock. *Who's there?*
Juno! *Juno who?*
I know who, do you know who?

92 **K**nock Knock. *Who's there?*
Jewell! *Jewell who?*
Jewell know me when you see me!

93 **K**nock Knock. *Who's there?*
Bashful! *Bashful who?*
I'm too shy to tell you!

94 **K**nock Knock. *Who's there?*
X! *X who?*
X-tremely pleased to meet you!

95 **K**nock Knock. *Who's there?*
C-2! *C-2 who?*
C-2 it that you don't forget my name next time!

96 **K**nock Knock. *Who's there?*
Albert! *Albert who?*
Albert you don't know who this is!

97 **K**nock Knock. *Who's there?*
Alex! *Alex who?*
Alex-plain later, just let me in!

98 **K**nock Knock. *Who's there?*
Lena! *Lena who?*
Lena little closer and I'll tell you!

99 **K**nock Knock. *Who's there?*
Ben! *Ben who?*
Ben down and look through the letter slot!

100 **K**nock Knock. *Who's there?*
Zeke! *Zeke who?*
Zeke and you shall find!

101 **K**nock Knock. *Who's there?*
Ellie! *Ellie who?*
Ellie-phants never forget!

102 **K**nock Knock. *Who's there?*
Kipper! *Kipper who?*
Kipper your hands off me!

103 **K**nock Knock. *Who's there?*
Dingo! *Dingo who?*
Dingo anywhere on the weekend!

104 **K**nock Knock. *Who's there?*
Orson! *Orson who?*
Orson cart!

105 **K**nock Knock. *Who's there?*
Roach! *Roach who?*
Roach you a letter but I didn't send it!

106 **K**nock Knock. *Who's there?*
Amos! *Amos who?*
Amosquito!

107 **K**nock Knock. *Who's there?*
Anna! *Anna who?*
Annather mosquito!

108 **K**nock Knock. *Who's there?*
Goose! *Goose who?*
Goosey Goosey Gander!

109 **K**nock Knock. *Who's there?*
Cattle! *Cattle who?*
Cattle always purr when you stroke it!

110 **K**nock Knock. *Who's there?*
Debate! *Debate who?*
Debate goes on de hook if you want to catch de fish!

111 **K**nock Knock. *Who's there?*
Bab! *Bab who?*
Baboons are a type of ape!

112 **K**nock Knock. *Who's there?*
Shamp! *Shamp who?*
Why, do I have lice?

113 **K**nock Knock. *Who's there?*
Adder! *Adder who?*
Adder you get in here?

114 **K**nock Knock. *Who's there?*
Lionel! *Lionel who?*
Lionel bite you if you don't watch out!

115 **K**nock Knock. *Who's there?*
Who! *Who who?*
What are you – an owl?

116 Knock Knock. Who's there?
Ocelot *Ocelot who?*
Ocelot of questions, don't you?

117 Knock Knock. *Who's there?*
Baby Owl! *Baby Owl who?*
Baby Owl see you later, maybe I won't!

118 Knock Knock. *Who's there?*
Rabbit! *Rabbit who?*
Rabbit up carefully, it's a present!

119 Knock Knock. *Who's there?*
Bark! *Bark who?*
Barking up the wrong tree!

120 Knock Knock. *Who's there?*
Don! *Don who?*
Donkey rides! Donkey rides! Only five dollars a ride!

121 Knock Knock. *Who's there?*
Gopher! *Gopher who?*
Gopher help, I've been tied up!

122 Knock Knock. *Who's there?*
Bear! *Bear who?*
Bearer of glad tidings!

123 Knock Knock. *Who's there?*
Althea! *Althea who?*
Althea later, alligator!

124 Knock Knock. *Who's there?*
Abbey! *Abbey who?*
Abbey hive is where honey is made!

125 Knock Knock. *Who's there?*
Caterpillar! *Caterpillar who?*
Cat-er-pillar of feline society!

126 Knock Knock. *Who's there?*
Bee! *Bee who?*
Bee careful!

127 Knock Knock. *Who's there?*
Cows go! *Cows go who?*
Cows go 'moo', not 'who'!

128 Knock Knock. *Who's there?*
My panther. *My panther who?*
My panther falling down!

129 Knock Knock. *Who's there?*
Teddy! *Teddy who?*
Teddy the neighbourhood, tomorrow the world!

130 Knock Knock. *Who's there?*
Celia! *Celia who?*
Celia later alligator!

131 Knock Knock. *Who's there?*
Quacker! *Quacker who?*
Quacker 'nother bad joke and I'm leaving!

132 Knock Knock. *Who's there?*
U-2! *U-2 who?*
U-2 can buy a brand-new car for only $199 a month!

133 Knock Knock. *Who's there?*
Carol! *Carol who?*
Carol go if you turn the ignition key!

134 Knock Knock. *Who's there?*
Colin! *Colin who?*
Colin all cars! Colin all cars!

135 Knock Knock. *Who's there?*
Cargo! *Cargo who?*
Cargo beep beep!

136 Knock Knock. *Who's there?*
Lisa! *Lisa who?*
Lisa new car, furniture or computer equipment!

137 Knock Knock. *Who's there?*
Carl! *Carl who?*
Carload of furniture for you! Where do you want it?

138 Knock Knock. *Who's there?*
Carlotta! *Carlotta who?*
Carlotta trouble when it breaks down!

139 Knock Knock. *Who's there?*
Utah! *Utah who?*
Utah the road and I'll mend the fence!

140 Knock Knock. *Who's there?*
Despair! *Despair who?*
Despair tyre is flat!

141 Knock Knock. *Who's there?*
Tank! *Tank who?*
You're welcome!

142 Knock Knock. *Who's there?*
Wenceslas! *Wenceslas who?*
Wenceslas bus home?

143 Knock Knock. *Who's there?*
Sal! *Sal who?*
Sal long way for me to go home!

144 Knock Knock. *Who's there?*
Datsun! *Datsun who?*
Datsun old joke!

145 Knock Knock. *Who's there?*
Sari! *Sari who?*
Sari I took so long!

146 Knock Knock. *Who's there?*
Sabina! *Sabina who?*
Sabina long time since I've been at your place!

147 Knock Knock. *Who's there?*
Mandy! *Mandy who?*
Mandy lifeboats, we're sinking!

148 Knock Knock. *Who's there?*
Rhoda! *Rhoda who?*
(sings) Row, Row, Rhoda boat!

149 Knock Knock. *Who's there?*
Abel! *Abel who?*
Abel seaman!

150 Knock Knock. *Who's there?*
Ben! *Ben who?*
Ben away a long time!

151 Knock Knock. *Who's there?*
Len! *Len who?*
Len me some money!

152 Knock Knock. *Who's there?*
Jo! *Jo who?*
Jo jump in the lake!

153 Knock Knock. *Who's there?*
Betty! *Betty who?*
Betty let me in or there'll be trouble!

154 Knock Knock. *Who's there?*
Canoe! *Canoe who?*
Canoe come out and play with me?

155 Knock Knock. *Who's there?*
Mister! *Mister who?*
Mister last train home!

156 Knock Knock. *Who's there?*
Betty! *Betty who?*
Betty late than never!

157 Knock Knock. *Who's there?*
Effie! *Effie who?*
Effie'd known you were coming he'd have stayed at home!

158 Knock Knock. *Who's there?*
Armageddon! *Armageddon who?*
Armageddon out of here!

159 Knock Knock. *Who's there?*
Shelby! *Shelby who?*
Shelby comin' round the mountain when she comes!

160 Knock Knock. *Who's there?*
Ida! *Ida who?*
Ida hard time getting here!

161 Knock Knock. *Who's there?*
Martha! *Martha who?*
Martha up to the top of the hill and marched them down again!

162 **K**nock Knock. *Who's there?*
Robin! *Robin who?*
Robin you, so hand over your cash!

163 **K**nock Knock. *Who's there?*
Justice! *Justice who?*
Justice I thought! You won't let me in!

164 **K**nock Knock. *Who's there?*
Bat! *Bat who?*
Batman and Robin are superheroes!

165 **K**nock Knock. *Who's there?*
Matt! *Matt who?*
Matter of fact!

166 **K**nock Knock. *Who's there?*
Police! *Police who?*
Police let me in!

167 **K**nock Knock. *Who's there?*
Foster! *Foster who?*
Foster than a speeding bullet!

168 **K**nock Knock. *Who's there?*
Ooze! *Ooze who?*
Ooze in charge around here?

169 **K**nock Knock. *Who's there?*
Gable! *Gable who?*
Gable to leap tall buildings in a single bound!

170 **K**nock Knock. *Who's there?*
Hijack! *Hijack who?*
Hi Jack! Where's Jill?

171 **K**nock Knock. *Who's there?*
Biafra! *Biafra who?*
Biafra'id, be very afraid!

172 **K**nock Knock. *Who's there?*
Witches. *Witches who?*
Witches the way home?

173 **K**nock Knock. *Who's there?*
Ogre! *Ogre who?*
Ogre the hill and far away!

174 **K**nock Knock. *Who's there?*
Voodoo! *Voodoo who?*
Voodoo you think you are?

175 **K**nock Knock. *Who's there?*
Wicked! *Wicked who?*
Wicked be a great couple
if you gave me a chance!

176 **K**nock Knock. *Who's there?*
Eliza! *Eliza who?*
Eliza wake at night thinking
about you!

177 **K**nock Knock. *Who's there?*
Manny! *Manny who?*
Manny are called, few
are chosen!

178 **K**nock Knock. *Who's there?*
Doctor! *Doctor who?*
That's right!

179 **K**nock Knock. *Who's there?*
Jess! *Jess who?*
Jess me and my shadow!

180 **K**nock Knock. *Who's there?*
Weirdo! *Weirdo who?*
Weirdo you think you're going?

181 **K**nock Knock. *Who's there?*
Fantasy! *Fantasy who?*
Fantasy a walk on the beach?

182 **K**nock Knock. *Who's there?*
Midas! *Midas who?*
Midas well let me in!

183 **K**nock Knock. *Who's there?*
Grant! *Grant who?*
Grant you three wishes!

184 **K**nock Knock. *Who's there?*
Zombies. *Zombies who?*
Zombies make honey, zombies
just buzz around.

185 **K**nock Knock. *Who's there?*
Irish! *Irish who?*
Irish I had a million dollars!

186 **K**nock Knock. *Who's there?*
Bridie! *Bridie who?*
Bridie light of the silvery moon!

187 **K**nock Knock. *Who's there?*
Mortimer! *Mortimer who?*
Mortimer than meets the eyes!

188 **K**nock Knock. *Who's there?*
Dan! *Dan who?*
Dan Druff!

189 **K**nock Knock. *Who's there?*
Abbey! *Abbey who?*
Abbey stung me on the nose!

190 **K**nock Knock. *Who's there?*
Knee! *Knee who?*
Knee-d you ask?

191 **K**nock Knock. *Who's there?*
Adair! *Adair who?*
Adair once, but I'm bald now!

192 **K**nock Knock. *Who's there?*
Hair! *Hair who?*
I'm hair to stay!

193 **K**nock Knock. *Who's there?*
Jaws! *Jaws who?*
Jaws truly!

194 **K**nock Knock. *Who's there?*
Meg! *Meg who?*
Meg up your own mind!

195 **K**nock Knock. *Who's there?*
Denise! *Denise who?*
Denise are between the waist and the feet!

196 **K**nock Knock. *Who's there?*
Hans! *Hans who?*
Hans are on the end of your arms!

197 **K**nock Knock. *Who's there?*
Jeff! *Jeff who?*
Jeff in one ear, can you please speak a bit louder!

198 **K**nock Knock. *Who's there?*
Nose! *Nose who?*
Nosey parker! Mind your own business!

199 **K**nock Knock. *Who's there?*
Disguise! *Disguise who?*
Disguise the limit!

200 **K**nock Knock. *Who's there?*
Butcher! *Butcher who?*
Butcher left leg in, butcher left leg out . . .

201 **K**nock Knock. *Who's there?*
Butcher! *Butcher who?*
Butcher little arms around me!

202 **K**nock Knock. *Who's there?*
Turnip! *Turnip who?*
Turnip for school tomorrow or there will be trouble!

203 **K**nock Knock. *Who's there?*
Adam! *Adam who?*
Adam up and tell me the total!

204 **K**nock Knock. *Who's there?*
Abe! *Abe who?*
Abe C D E F G H!

205 **K**nock Knock. *Who's there?*
Dad! *Dad who?*
Dad 2 and 2 to get 4!

206 **K**nock Knock. *Who's there?*
Ella! *Ella who?*
Ella-mentary, my dear fellow!

207 **K**nock Knock. *Who's there?*
Lois! *Lois who?*
Lois the opposite of high!

208 **K**nock Knock. *Who's there?*
Oscar! *Oscar who?*
Oscar silly question, get a silly answer!

209 **K**nock Knock. *Who's there?*
Diego! *Diego who?*
Diegos before the B!

210 **K**nock Knock. *Who's there?*
Juan! *Juan who?*
(sings) Juan two three o'clock, four o'clock rock!

211 **K**nock Knock. *Who's there?*
Norma Lee! *Norma Lee who?*
Norma Lee I'd be at school but I've got the day off!

212 **K**nock Knock. *Who's there?*
Pencil! *Pencil who?*
Pencil fall down if you don't wear a belt!

213 **K**nock Knock. *Who's there?*
Percy! *Percy who?*
Percy vere and you'll go a long way!

214 **K**nock Knock. *Who's there?*
Mike and Angelo! *Mike and Angelo who?*
Mike and Angelo was a great sculptor!

215 Knock Knock. *Who's there?*
Irish stew! *Irish stew who?*
Irish stew in the name of the law!

216 Knock Knock. *Who's there?*
Beck! *Beck who?*
Beckfast is ready!

217 Knock Knock. *Who's there?*
Renata! *Renata who?*
Renata milk, can you spare a cup?

218 Knock Knock. *Who's there?*
Justin! *Justin who?*
Justin time for lunch!

219 Knock Knock. *Who's there?*
Phil! *Phil who?*
Phil my glass up to the rim!

220 Knock Knock. *Who's there?*
Wanda! *Wanda who?*
Wanda buy some cookies?

221 Knock Knock. *Who's there?*
Beef! *Beef who?*
Beefair now!

222 Knock Knock. *Who's there?*
Noah! *Noah who?*
Noah counting for taste!

223 Knock Knock. *Who's there?*
U-8! *U-8 who?*
U-8 my lunch!

224 Knock Knock. *Who's there?*
Beet! *Beet who?*
Beets me! I've forgotten my own name!

225 Knock Knock. *Who's there?*
Arthur! *Arthur who?*
Arthur any more jelly beans in the jar?

226 Knock Knock. *Who's there?*
Patty! *Patty who?*
Patty cake, patty cake, baker's man!

227 Knock Knock. *Who's there?*
Xenia! *Xenia who?*
Xenia stealing my candy!

228 Knock Knock. *Who's there?*
Abba! *Abba who?*
Abba banana!

229 Knock Knock. *Who's there?*
Bernadette! *Bernadette who?*
Bernadette my lunch!
Now I'm starving!

230 Knock Knock. *Who's there?*
Cook! *Cook who?*
One o'clock!

231 Knock Knock. *Who's there?*
Barbie! *Barbie who?*
Barbie Q!

232 Knock Knock. *Who's there?*
Euripides! *Euripides who?*
Euripides pants, Eumenides pants!

233 Knock Knock. *Who's there?*
Carmen! *Carmen who?*
Carmen get it!

234 Knock Knock. *Who's there?*
Noah! *Noah who?*
Noah yes? What's your decision?

235 Knock Knock. *Who's there?*
Caesar! *Caesar who?*
Caesar jolly good fellow!

236 Knock Knock. *Who's there?*
Ben Hur! *Ben Hur who?*
Ben Hur almost an hour so let me in!

237 Knock Knock. *Who's there?*
Red! *Red who?*
Knock Knock. *Who's there?*
Red! *Red who?*
Knock Knock. *Who's there?*
Red! *Red who?*
Knock Knock. *Who's there?*
Red! *Red who?*
Knock Knock. *Who's there?*
Orange! *Orange who?*
Orange you glad I didn't say red?

238 Knock Knock. *Who's there?*
Caesar! *Caesar who?*
Caesar quickly, before she gets away!

239 Knock Knock. *Who's there?*
Jester! *Jester who?*
Jester minute! I'm looking for my key!

240 Knock Knock. *Who's there?*
Mickey! *Mickey who?*
Mickey is stuck in the lock!

241 Knock Knock. *Who's there?*
Chuck! *Chuck who?*
Chuck if I've left my keys inside!

242 **K**nock Knock. *Who's there?*
Xavier! *Xavier who?*
Xavier money for a rainy day!

243 **K**nock Knock. *Who's there?*
Ken! *Ken who?*
Ken I come in? It's raining!

244 **K**nock Knock. *Who's there?*
Sombrero. *Sombrero who?*
Sombrero-ver the rainbow . . .

245 **K**nock Knock. *Who's there?*
Lee King! *Lee King who?*
Lee King bucket!

246 **K**nock Knock. *Who's there?*
Gary! *Gary who?*
Gary on smiling!

247 **K**nock Knock. *Who's there?*
Boo! *Boo who?*
What are you crying about?

248 **K**nock Knock. *Who's there?*
Boo! *Boo who?*
Here's a hanky, now let me in!

249 **K**nock Knock. *Who's there?*
Barbara! *Barbara who?*
Barbara black sheep, have you any wool . . .

250 **K**nock Knock. *Who's there?*
Alison! *Alison who?*
Alison to the radio!

251 **K**nock Knock. *Who's there?*
Lucinda! *Lucinda who?*
(sings) Lucinda sky with diamonds!

252 **K**nock Knock. *Who's there?*
Ike! *Ike who?*
(sings) Ike could have danced all night!

253 **K**nock Knock. *Who's there?*
Harmony! *Harmony who?*
Harmony electricians does it take to change a light bulb?

254 **K**nock Knock. *Who's there?*
Accordion! *Accordion who?*
Accordion to the TV, it's going to rain tomorrow!

255 **K**nock Knock. *Who's there?*
Oboe! *Oboe who?*
Oboe, I've got the wrong house!

256 **K**nock Knock. *Who's there?*
Jasmine! *Jasmine who?*
Jasmine play the saxophone, piano and trumpet!

257 Knock Knock. *Who's there?*
Europe! *Europe who?*
Europen the door so I can come in!

258 Knock Knock. *Who's there?*
Cologne! *Cologne who?*
Cologne me names won't get you anywhere!

259 Knock Knock. *Who's there?*
Genoa! *Genoa who?*
Genoa good place to have a meal around here?

260 Knock Knock. *Who's there?*
Norway! *Norway who?*
Norway am I leaving until I've spoken to you!

261 Knock Knock. *Who's there?*
Kent! *Kent who?*
Kent you let me in?

262 Knock Knock. *Who's there?*
Tibet! *Tibet who?*
Early Tibet, early to rise!

263 Knock Knock. *Who's there?*
Abyssinia! *Abyssinia who?*
Abyssinia when I get back!

264 Knock Knock. *Who's there?*
Parish! *Parish who?*
Parish is the capital of France!

265 Knock Knock. *Who's there?*
Francis! *Francis who?*
Francis the home of the Eiffel Tower!

266 Knock Knock. *Who's there?*
Iran! *Iran who?*
Iran 30 laps around the track and I'm very tired now!

267 Knock Knock. *Who's there?*
Troy! *Troy who?*
Troy as I may, I can't reach the bell!

268 Knock Knock. *Who's there?*
Jamaica! *Jamaica who?*
Jamaica mistake!

269 Knock Knock. *Who's there?*
Kenya! *Kenya who?*
Kenya keep the noise down, some of us are trying to sleep!

270 Knock Knock. *Who's there?*
Java! *Java who?*
Java dollar you can lend me?

271 **K**nock Knock. *Who's there?*
Bella! *Bella who?*
Bella bottom trousers!

272 **K**nock Knock. *Who's there?*
Nobel! *Nobel who?*
No bell so I just knocked!

273 **K**nock Knock. *Who's there?*
Pier! *Pier who?*
Pier through the peephole and you'll see!

274 **K**nock Knock. *Who's there?*
Paula! *Paula who?*
Paula nother one! It's got bells on it!

275 **K**nock Knock. *Who's there?*
Ima! *Ima who?*
Ima going home if you don't let me in!

276 **K**nock Knock. *Who's there?*
Abbot! *Abbot who?*
Abbot time you opened this door!

277 **K**nock Knock. *Who's there?*
Figs! *Figs who?*
Figs the doorbell, it's been broken for ages!

278 **K**nock Knock. *Who's there?*
Jethro! *Jethro who?*
Jethro a rope out the window!

279 **K**nock Knock. *Who's there?*
Des! *Des who?*
Des no bell! That's why I'm knocking!

280 **K**nock Knock. *Who's there?*
Diss! *Diss who?*
Diss is ridiculous! Let me in!

281 **K**nock Knock. *Who's there?*
Mabel! *Mabel who?*
Mabel doesn't work either!

282 **K**nock Knock. *Who's there?*
Sherwood! *Sherwood who?*
Sherwood love to come inside! How about it?

283 **K**nock Knock. *Who's there?*
Miniature! *Miniature who?*
Miniature let me in I'll tell you!

284 **K**nock Knock. *Who's there?*
Evan! *Evan who?*
Evan you should know who I am!

285 **K**nock Knock. *Who's there?*
Still! *Still who?*
Still knocking!

286 **K**nock Knock. *Who's there?*
Gus! *Gus who?*
No, you guess who.
I already know!

287 **K**nock Knock. *Who's there?*
Welcome! *Welcome who?*
Welcome outside and join me!

288 **K**nock Knock. *Who's there?*
Howard! *Howard who?*
Howard I know?

289 **K**nock Knock. *Who's there?*
Sarah! *Sarah who?*
Sarah nother way in?

290 **K**nock Knock. *Who's there?*
Shirley! *Shirley who?*
Shirley you know by now!

291 **K**nock Knock. *Who's there?*
Pa! *Pa who?*
Pa-don me! Can I come in?

292 **K**nock Knock. *Who's there?*
Scott! *Scott who?*
Scott nothing to do with you!

293 **K**nock Knock. *Who's there?*
Sally! *Sally who?*
Sally duffer! It's just me!

294 **K**nock Knock. *Who's there?*
Neil! *Neil who?*
Neil down and take a look!

295 **K**nock Knock. *Who's there?*
Offer! *Offer who?*
Offer gotten who I am!

296 **K**nock Knock. *Who's there?*
Celeste! *Celeste who?*
Celeste time I come around here!

297 **K**nock Knock.
Who's there?
Nobody!
Nobody who?
No body, just a skeleton!

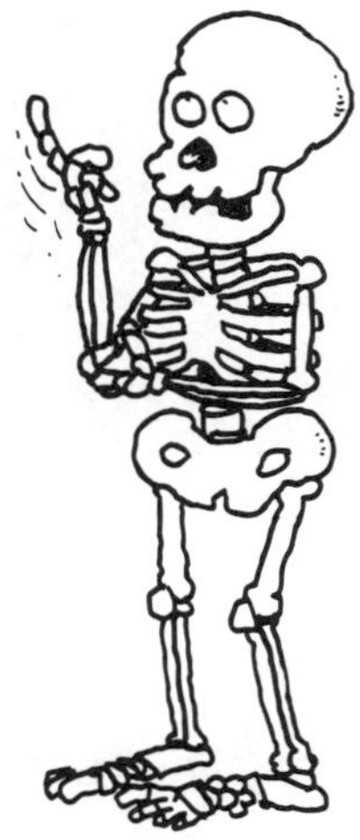

298 **K**nock Knock. *Who's there?*
Pasture! *Pasture who?*
Pasture bedtime, isn't it?

299 **K**nock Knock. *Who's there?*
Rose! *Rose who?*
Rose early to come and see you!

300 **K**nock Knock. *Who's there?*
Lillian! *Lillian who?*
Lillian the garden!

301 **K**nock Knock. *Who's there?*
Leif! *Leif who?*
Leif me alone!

302 **K**nock Knock. *Who's there?*
Reed! *Reed who?*
Reed-turn to sender!

303 **K**nock Knock. *Who's there?*
Weed! *Weed who?*
Weed better mow the lawn before it gets too long.

304 **K**nock Knock. *Who's there?*
Nicholas! *Nicholas who?*
Nicholas girls shouldn't climb trees!

305 **K**nock Knock. *Who's there?*
Roxanne! *Roxanne who?*
Roxanne pebbles are all over your garden!

306 **K**nock Knock. *Who's there?*
Wayne! *Wayne who?*
Wayne, Wayne, go away, come again another day!

307 **K**nock Knock. *Who's there?*
Theresa! *Theresa who?*
Theresa green!

308 **K**nock Knock. *Who's there?*
Woodward! *Woodward who?*
Woodward have come but he was busy!

309 **K**nock Knock. *Who's there?*
Woody! *Woody who?*
Woody now be a good time to visit?

310 **K**nock Knock. *Who's there?*
House! *House who?*
House it going?

311 **K**nock Knock. *Who's there?*
Barry! *Barry who?*
Barry the treasure where no one will find it!

312 **K**nock Knock. *Who's there?*
Haden! *Haden who?*
Haden seek!

313 **K**nock Knock. *Who's there?*
Tuba. *Tuba who?*
Tuba toothpaste.

314 **K**nock Knock. *Who's there?*
Moppet! *Moppet who?*
Moppet up before someone slips!

315 **K**nock Knock. *Who's there?*
Lucy! *Lucy who?*
Lucy lastic is embarrassing!

316 **K**nock Knock. *Who's there?*
Matthew! *Matthew who?*
Matthew lace has come undone!

317 **K**nock Knock. *Who's there?*
Waiter! *Waiter who?*
Waiter minute while I tie my shoe.

318 **K**nock Knock. *Who's there?*
Dwayne! *Dwayne who?*
Dwayne the bathtub before I drown!

319 **K**nock Knock. *Who's there?*
Wooden shoe! *Wooden shoe who?*
Wooden shoe like to know!

320 **K**nock Knock. *Who's there?*
Gladys! *Gladys who?*
Gladys Saturday, aren't you?

321 **K**nock Knock. *Who's there?*
Tamara! *Tamara who?*
Tamara is Wednesday, today is Tuesday!

322 **K**nock Knock. *Who's there?*
Wednesday! *Wednesday who?*
(sings) Wednesday saints go marching in!

323 **K**nock Knock. *Who's there?*
You! *You who?*
Did you call?

324 **K**nock Knock. *Who's there?*
Who! *Who who?*
I can hear an echo!

325 Knock Knock. *Who's there?*
Closure! *Closure who?*
Closure mouth when you're eating!

326 Knock Knock. *Who's there?*
Carrie! *Carrie who?*
Carrie on with what you're doing!

327 Knock Knock. *Who's there?*
Icon! *Icon who?*
Icon tell you another Knock Knock joke! Do you want me to?

328 Knock Knock. *Who's there?*
Avenue! *Avenue who?*
Avenue heard these jokes before?

329 Knock Knock. *Who's there?*
Dishes! *Dishes who?*
Dishes a very bad joke!

330 Knock Knock. *Who's there?*
Hugo! *Hugo who?*
Hugo one way, I'll go the other!

331 Knock Knock. *Who's there?*
Mary! *Mary who?*
Mary Christmas and a happy new year!

332 Knock Knock. *Who's there?*
Danielle! *Danielle who?*
Danielle so loud, I can hear you!

333 Knock Knock. *Who's there?*
Watson! *Watson who?*
Watson TV tonight?

334 Knock Knock. *Who's there?*
Samantha! *Samantha who?*
Samantha others have already gone!

335 Knock Knock. *Who's there?*
Beth! *Beth who?*
Beth wisheth, thweetie!

336 Knock Knock. *Who's there?*
Ines! *Ines who?*
Ines second I'm going to turn around and go home!

337 Knock Knock. *Who's there?*
Irish! *Irish who?*
Irish I knew some more Knock Knock jokes.

338 Knock Knock. *Who's there?*
Hester! *Hester who?*
Hester la vista!

339 Knock Knock. *Who's there?*
Dat! *Dat who?*
Dat's all folks!

Ridiculous Rhymes

1 My teacher

My teacher doesn't eat; she doesn't scratch or fart,
She never, ever even has a drink.
She never sneezes, burps or laughs,
And I've never even seen her try to blink.

Even though she wears no shoes,
She still squeaks when she walks.
And her mouth never seems to move,
Even when she talks.

I thought she was an alien,
But now I think she's not.
She's not a very useful one,
But I think she's a robot!

2

There once was a boy from France,
Who found some baked beans by chance.
He ate them so quickly,
That soon he felt sickly,
And blew a great hole in his pants.

A is for apple, crunchy and firm, Just hope you never see half a worm.
B is for Brussels sprouts, the worst food ever seen, If your parents make you eat them, they're just mean.

3 Killer bunnies

Beware killer bunnies, for although they look sweet,
They're really just looking for raw guts to eat.
They have metal spikes that shoot out of their paws,
So protect your guts, or they might eat yours!

They wriggle their bunny noses, and twitch their bunny ears,
Then they get in killer bunny fights and cause lots of tears.
They pretend to be cute, but that's just a trick,
As soon as you turn your back they'll give your butt a kick.

They will headbutt babies, they will eye-gouge grannies,
They will tease other bunnies and they will poop on nannies.
They will bite your nose, and they will scratch your eyes,
So I recommend you get them first, and make lots of rabbit pies.

4 Things

Things can get messy if you're juggling chainsaws,
Things can get boring if there's too long a ... pause.
Things can get smelly if you stand behind a cow,
Things can get ugly if the wind changes now.

Things can get wet if there's no toilet nearby,
Things can get embarrassing if you don't do up your fly.
Things can get snotty if you're picking your nose,
Things can get fungal if you don't clean your toes.

Things can get stinky if you don't take a shower,
Things can get thorny if you eat the wrong flower.
Things can get gross if your farts come out runny,
And I can get sacked if this poem isn't funny.

C is for cockroaches, scuttling along, In a nuclear explosion, nothing lives as long.

5 There once was a girl named Rose,
Who had quite peculiar toes.
If she bent the right way,
At the right time of day,
She could use them for picking her nose.

6 Ears

Some people have big ears, sticking right out,
Others have small ears in which you must shout.
Some people have earlobes which hang very low,
Others have ears from which hair will grow.
The only real worry, it must be said,
Is if your ears are anywhere
But the side of your head.

7 A painful day

Today was painful, not at all nice,
I stepped on a trap that was meant for the mice.
It snapped on my toes, making me scream,
With eyes closed, I stumbled, straight through the fly screen.

I stepped on a broken bottle, cut my foot on the glass,
Slipped on some dog poo and fell on my … bum.
I slowly stood up, in a fair bit of pain,
Then stepped on a rake, it was insane!

I went inside, to get help and first aid,
And maybe a soothing glass of lemonade.
But to top off my day, Mum got all shirty,
And yelled at me for making the carpet all dirty!

D is for dogs, cute and sweet, Until they decide to poo in the street.

8 There once was a boy aged four,
Who knocked his dad straight to the floor.
I'm afraid it all started,
When the young fellow farted,
And the smell was rotten to the core.

9 What pet should I get?

Don't get a bear, they sleep all winter,
Don't get a cheetah unless you're a sprinter.
Don't get a bull, they like to charge,
Don't get an elephant, they're way too large.

Don't get a vampire bat, they suck too much blood.
Don't get a cow because they chew too much cud.
If you don't want something lazy, don't get a sloth,
If you haven't got lights, don't get a moth.

Don't get a skink, they keep losing their tails,
And if you want a small pet, forget about whales.
They're a popular fish, but don't get a guppy,
Hang on – it's simple: just get a puppy!

10 The world's worst pirate

Once upon a time, in a town by the sea,
Lived a fierce pirate named Captain Trevor.
Well, I say 'fierce', but if we face facts,
Captain Trevor was the worst pirate ever.

He didn't like sailing; he was allergic to salt,
The smallest wave made him want to spew.
He tried recruiting, but he was so bad,
He was the only man in his crew.

He tried raiding a ship, fired one cannon shot,
But to do that you need to be clever.
Captain Trevor had the cannon back to front,
And that was the end of the worst pirate ever.

11 There once was a girl named Clare,
Who had more snot than really was fair.
She went in for a pick,
But the snot was too thick,
And her finger got stuck up in there.

E is for elephants, with trunks that sway, But if they farted they'd blow you away.

12 Things that shouldn't go together

Superman and kryptonite,
Thunderstorms and dogs.
Monster trucks and fairies,
Blow flies and frogs.

Teddy bears and blenders,
Barbie dolls and knives.
Cabbage Patch Kids and microwaves,
Ken dolls and wives.

Now they aren't all the things,
That shouldn't go together.
But if I tried to list them all,
Then we'd be here forever.

13 My friend Marco

My friend Marco can sleep anywhere,
At any time of day.
He fell asleep in a football match,
Just after we started to play.

He fell asleep in front of the telly,
He fell asleep at the zoo.
He fell asleep at school, in maths,
And he fell asleep on the loo!

He fell asleep riding his bike;
He fell asleep down a drain.
I hope and I hope when he gets a job,
That it isn't flying a plane!

F is for feet, which aren't gross, you wouldn't think, Unless they are warty with bunions and stink.

14

There once was a girl named Michelle,
Who had trouble choosing hardware well.
So without restraint,
She bought stripy paint,
And a left-handed hammer as well.

15 I'm freaking out

Spiders freak me out because they're really freaky,
Robbers freak me out because they're really sneaky.
Yahtzee freaks me out because there are so many dice,
Head scratchers freak me out … I think that they have lice.

Heights freak me out because if I fell I would die,
Fingers freak me out because they poke me in the eye.
Frogs freak me out because their tongues are so long,
Gorillas freak me out because I've seen King Kong.

16 Do you gurgle when you gargle?

Do you gurgle when you gargle?
Do you giggle when you fart?
Do you grumble when you're grumpy?
Do you appreciate fine art?

Do you blow your nose when it's itchy,
Or prefer to have a pick?
If you don't want to go to school,
Do you pretend that you are sick?

Do you think the things I've mentioned?
Do you do the things I've said?
If you do, it's good, in fact it's great,
Because it means that you're not dead.

17 There once was a man named Zeke,
Who thought he had reached his peak.
But he was such a bore,
That people would snore,
As soon as he started to speak.

G is for garbage, which is no surprise, It has to be gross if it gets eaten by flies.

18 Whacky words

If you hear a borborygmus, you might want to eat,
And if you want to skedaddle, start moving your feet.
If an illywhacker hornswoggles you, that's really not fair,
And if you are glabrous, you have no hair.

A slubberdegullion will often pandiculate,
Dysania strikes, always making them late.
I tell you no furphies, this is all true,
What? You're not flabbergasted now, are you?

Don't talk to flibbertigibbets, tell them to beat it,
And masticate all your food when you eat it.
Relax, when I say 'masticate' I'm not being rude,
It's simply to do with chewing your food.

19 Asparagus

There are things Mum makes me eat,
That I do not like, that are not sweet.
Mum loves asparagus, so we eat it all the time.
Favourite foods? Asparagus is *so* not one of mine!

It's green and gross and the taste is so yuck,
That every time I eat it, it makes me want to chuck.
I mix it with mashed potatoes, and smother it in sauce,
I do not know why she serves it up with every single course.

Asparagus dip and biscuits, steamed asparagus with pie,
Asparagus-flavoured ice-cream, too – I think that I might die!
I eat all this asparagus, and I do not feel mellow,
Especially the next day when my wee stinks and is yellow!

H is for Harriet, a girl on my street, Who likes to pick her nose, then have it to eat.

20 There once was a girl up a tree,
Who was pleased with how far she could see.
But a bird gave her a peck,
A squirrel bit her neck,
And then she got stung by a bee.

21 Swimming

I love to go swimming in the swimming pool,
But something happened that was not cool!
I swallowed some water, which made me bellow,
Because I was in a patch that was warm and yellow.
I don't know who it was, but they forgot the number one rule:
Dude, we don't swim in your toilet, so don't pee in our pool!

22 The doctor

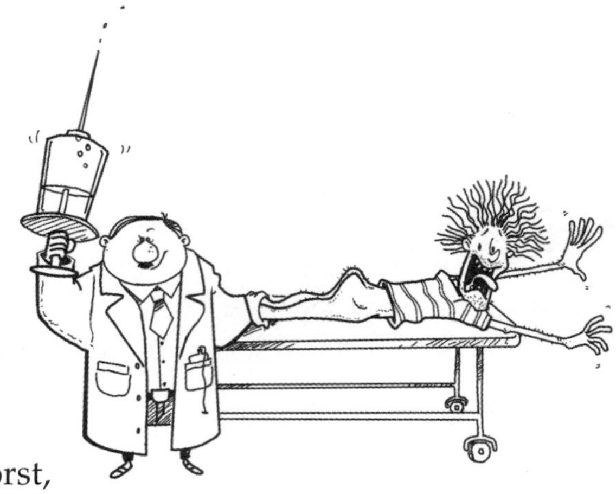

There are two awful places that I don't like to go,
If you've been there you'll understand,
you'll sympathise, you'll know.
The doctor and the dentist, they really are the worst,
But in worstness terms – if that's a word – the doctor sure comes first.

Injections hurt, lozenges suck,
Medicine tastes really yuck.
Thermometers are super cold, but of the two options I've got,
Under my arm is my preferred thermometer-placing spot.

I don't like the way the doctor wears a crisp white coat,
I don't like taking tablets when they get stuck in my throat.
The only good thing, I suppose, is when they finally stop,
Even though I'm nearly 12, I still get a lollipop!

I is for itchy, which is gross to some, Especially if that itch is right on your bum.

23 There once was a dinosaur named Fred,
Who was dumb, it has to be said.
He thought, 'I really do think,
It's better to be extinct,
Than for all the dinosaurs to be dead.'

24 The outdoor cinema

I went to an outdoor cinema; I thought it would be nice,
But I will not be going to that wretched place twice.
We had a picnic, then got ready for the movie,
When something horrid happened that wasn't
very groovy.

Twilight fell and the bats came out in flight,
It really was quite an interesting sight.
But then one bat, flying directly overhead,
Let one go and pooped directly on my head!

25 Chores

I have to tell you that my parents are quite cheap,
Here are the chores they make me do for just five bucks a week:
I vacuum the house, I make my bed and do the dishes as well,
I have to pick up all the dog poo and boy, that stuff can smell!

I clean my room, I pick up my clothes, even the old socks,
Although, when they've been there for a while, I use tongs for the dirty jocks.
I use the net to get the leaves out of our swimming pool,
I walk Rover in the morning, and I walk him after school.

I brush our long-haired cat, to get out the knots, you see,
Then what does that stupid, snobby cat do? She goes and scratches me!
So they are the chores I have to do, and it really isn't fair;
If I got paid what I'm really worth, I'd be a millionaire!

J is for jumping, if you're jumping in bare feet, And your dog has just done a dog poo in the street.

26 There once was a girl named Claire,
Who never, ever cut her hair.
When she turned 21,
It was way past her bum,
And three birds were nesting in there.

27 Opposites

Ice-cream is yummy, but Brussels sprouts are yuck,
It's great to blow bubbles but you wouldn't want to suck.
Jam doughnuts can be hot, meat pies can be cold,
Fruit is nice when it's new, but mouldy when it's old.

I love patting dogs, I hate getting a mosquito bite,
I always get confused between my left hand and my right.
Circles are round, and squares are square,
Hairy heads are hairy, bald heads have no hair.

It takes time to climb up, but it's quick to fall back down,
When you're happy you will smile, when you're sooky
you will frown.
You finish at the end after starting at the start,
And you can do a silent but deadly, or a loud but friendly, fart.

28 Being scared

I'm scared of high heights and I'm scared of big dogs,
I'm scared of being squashed; I'm scared of frogs.
There's a girl at school I'm scared of, her name is Tilly,
But some of the things I'm scared of, well, they're just really silly.

I'm scared of milkshake makers, I'm scared of baked beans,
I'm scared of polka-dot dresses and I'm scared of fax machines.
I'm scared of yellow sticky notes, I'm scared of Bronwen's burp,
When I eat a bowl of soup, I'm scared that I will slurp.

I'm scared of animals in clothes, I'm scared of chocolate spreads,
I'm scared of TV remote controls and I'm scared of men's bald heads.
I'm scared of foot massages, and I'm scared of being dared,
But most of all I think that I'm just scared of being scared.

K is for karaoke, which is just all wrong, Especially when a big guy sings a Britney song.

29

There once was a caveman named Omar,
Who was sick of walking so far.
He invented the wheel,
Cried, 'This is unreal!
Now someone invent me a car!'

30 I've got a feeling

I've got a feeling,
It doesn't feel good,
I think it's a gas attack
Under my hood.

Rank and putrid,
Foul and smelly,
The kind of fart
That hurts my belly!

31 Snot

It comes in colours of all different sorts,
It goes out with your blows and back in with your snorts.
Dry and hard, wet and sticky, or even in a clot,
Yep, you guessed it – you're spot on – we're talking about snot!

When you're small you might have a pick,
Get out some snot and give it a lick.
Once you're older and more mature by far,
You can pick it at the lights in your fancy work car.

When you sneeze, snot goes flying,
But it dribbles out slow and thick when you're crying.
Hold one nostril, and blow with the other,
And you might shoot snot all over your brother.

L is for loogeys, which gross me out, Especially if someone hoicks one up, then spits it out.

32 There once was a massive beast,
That weighed 20 tonnes at least.
Some cavemen caught him,
And when they brought him
Home it was a four-week feast.

33 Television

I watch so much television, my mum tries
To tell me that I'll end up with big square eyes.
But I love all that TV every week,
And if I end up with square eyes, at least I'll look unique.

34 My Dad snores

My Dad snores, it makes me weep,
Because it means I can never sleep.
I've stuck corks up his nostrils, and pegs on his nose,
I've held his hand but the snore just grows.

I've sung lullabies for hours, and I've rocked his bed,
I've snuck brandy in his coffee, and whisky in his bread.
I've brought him a blanket, to help keep him warm,
But still he sounds like a thunderstorm.

I gave up then, I'd had enough,
Stopping this noise was way too tough.
Then, the answer, the end of my tears,
If I couldn't stop him snoring, I'd stick plugs in my ears!

35 There once was a caveman named Bradley,
Who wanted hot food really badly.
So he invented fire,
Which you have to admire,
But then he burnt his fingers, quite sadly.

M is for mould, which, it must be said, Is not good to see on the last bite of bread.

36 I'm still freaking out

Lightning freaks me out if I'm not wearing rubber shoes,
Wallabies freak me out but not as much as kangaroos.
Identical twins freak me out, they're like one person times two,
And chocolate spreads freak me out because they look like
runny poo.

Babies freak me out because they're wrinkly and tiny,
Glitter freaks me out because it's way too shiny.
Rabbits freak me out because they have so many babies,
Rats freak me out because I think that they have rabies.

37 If you ever...

If you ever get the chance to see a monkey dance,
Or a lion gets a notion to mix a magic potion,
Or a dog thinks it'd be great to get his board out for a skate,
Or a tiger thinks it's time to start performing mime,
Or an elephant decides to go on scary rides,
Or a snake whose name is Luke gets sick and has a puke,
Or a wombat thinks it's cool to play poker with a mule,
Or the paper's being read by a bear with a sore head,
Or a crocodile needs its toes to pick its snotty nose,
Or a tiny little mouse blows up his neighbour's house,
Or a giraffe that's pretty tall, decides to juggle one ball …
then 2 … then 3 … then 23 ...
TAKE A PHOTO! This may never ever, ever, ever happen again.

N is for nappies, which do their job well, But when they've been used, whoa! What a smell.

38 There once was a werewolf named Scott,
Who howled at the moon quite a lot.
But he was such a dunce,
That he bit himself once,
And needed a rabies shot.

39 Babies

Babies are cute, or so people say,
But I tend to see things another way.
All my baby sister seems to do is cry,
And do things that smell so bad I think that I might die.
At least, I suppose, when it's her they all adore,
I get away with heaps more stuff than I ever did before.

40 Laughing

You see something funny; a smile starts to form.
The thing gets funnier; your smile gets more warm.
It gets funnier still; you start a small snicker.
Funnier, funnier, your snicker gets quicker.

Now it's a giggle, although not for long,
Because soon a chuckle will come along.
A belly laugh next, which becomes a guffaw,
You're laughing so much that you fall on the floor.

Now your laugh stops, there are tears on your face;
A big laugh like that is just great, really ace.
So laugh and laugh and laugh and laugh,
And laugh and laugh and laugh and LAUGH!

O is for octopi or however it's said, It's gross to have eight sucking legs on your head.

41 There once was a vampire named Wally,
Who thought biting necks was pure folly.
Yep, this vampire dud,
Hated sucking blood,
He'd rather suck a sugar-free lolly.

42 Socks and sandals

Mum makes me wear socks with sandals,
'Cause she's worried my toes will get cold.
Well that's fine for her; she's not the one,
Who's dressed like they're 80 years old.

What next, Mum? Brown pants pulled up high?
I bet you'd be happy with that.
And I suppose when I go with you in the car,
You'd like me to wear a felt hat?

You'll get me a walking frame and a set of false teeth,
On mashed corn you'll make me dine.
This is what socks and sandals will lead to,
For crying out loud, Mum, I'm 9!

43 A day at the theme park

I go to the theme park and take my emotions on a roller coaster.
There are more ups than downs, but we finish at the start.
It's disappointing when I order a hot dog and get a sausage in a roll.
A long-haired terrier on a 30 degree day would have been better.
When the lady gives me my food I bite her hand.
She isn't too happy about it.
My drink is either just over half full or just below half empty, I'm not sure.
The guy at the ride punches my ticket, so I punch him.
I claim it was a protective instinct.
When asked if I can leave, I climb a tree, hang from
a branch, turn brown and fall out.

P is for pigs, which are smart, but, They spend their day rolling around in the mud.

44 There was a monster named Frankenstein,
Who thought things were going just fine.
But when he gave a cough,
His head came clean off,
'Cause his bolts had been loose for some time.

45 Soccer

Mum made me play soccer,
(Also called football).
And I tell you straight, right here, right now,
I did not like it at all.

I fell in the mud and got all dirty,
Then I got kicked in the shin.
I tried to kick the ball away from our goal,
But instead I kicked it straight in.

I tried heading the ball but it hit my nose,
I got a black eye and lump on my head.
I begged Mum to let me stop playing soccer,
So she signed me up for boxing instead!

46 Werewolves

Some people seem just like you and me,
Except in black and white they see.
They eat steak for dinner, just like we do,
But they have it raw! Chuck, chunder, spew!

It's when the moon is full that they become really scary,
They grow a tail, paws and fangs, and become really hairy.
They stare at the moon and howl great big howls,
And they have lots of drool dribbling out of their jowls.

Now they like to eat cows, and chickens too,
And if you don't watch out, they might eat you.
So when that moon's all round and wide,
Just make sure that you're safe inside.

Q is for queasy, which is how I feel, If I hear this poem while I'm eating my meal.

47 There once was a vampire named Bec,
Who threw up her hands and said, 'Heck!'
Then she started to bawl,
'I have no friends at all,
Because I'm a pain in the neck!'

48 Jason's pets

My friend Jason has pets galore,
He asked if I wanted to see them. I said, 'Sure.'
His dog peed on my leg so I tried to give it a spank,
But it jumped out of my reach and into the piranha tank.

Bubbles, blood, a total disaster,
I've never, ever seen a dog eaten faster.
Jason almost cried, but saved that for later,
First he introduced me to his pet alligator.

I looked in close – it was in a dark place,
Then the alligator tried to bite off my face!
It missed but still had a snack, I fear,
'Cause ever since that day I've had only one ear.

49 Getting gassy is...

To pass wind,
To have a small explosion between one's legs,
To be silent but deadly,
To be loud but friendly,
To kill seven in one blow,
To wilt flowers,
To warm the bed,
To risk follow through,
To prove hot air rises,
To unleash the great gas monster...

R is for rats, which sometimes have scabies, If they're frothing at the mouth they probably have rabies.

To fluff,
To give a Dutch oven,
To play the butt trumpet,
To bottom burp,
To destroy the ozone layer,
To set off a stealth bomber,
To pfft,
To be tight and squeaky,
To be loose and rumbly,
To hit seven on the Richter scale...

50 There once was a boy named Zeke,
Who blew a bubble the size of his cheek.
When it popped it was sticky,
And gooey and icky,
And he had gum in his hair for a week.

51 Bike riding

I ride so fast my eyes get teary,
I ride so far my legs get weary.
Sometimes I crash, and get all bloody,
Or I ride through puddles, and get all muddy.

I try and do jumps, sometimes they work,
Sometimes I stack and look like a jerk.
Mum says that I should try and go slow,
But she doesn't ride bikes, so she doesn't know.

S is for socks, which usually are ace, You just don't want an old pair rubbed in your face.

52 Their once was a girl named Mel,
And buoy, did she like two spell.
She red a dictionary each knight,
Too bee shore words were write,
And eye think she spelled really well.

53 The close talker

I was talking to someone the other night,
And the way they talked gave me a fright.
They talked so close, so I could hear,
But they breathed directly into my ear.

They'd eaten chips, so when they said what they said,
Little bits of food bounced off my head.
This was out of control – they were way too near,
But the final straw was when they accidentally licked my ear.

'Enough!' I shouted. 'Enough close talking from you!
Just back away from me, I feel like I will spew.
I'm going to go somewhere that I can be alone,
And if you still want to talk to me, call me on the phone!'

54 My dog, Bill

I used to play with my dog Bill,
Until one day he made a kill.
The cat was trying to play a game,
But Bill thought that the game was lame.

Bill bit the cat and made it dead,
By biting it right on the head.
He crunched its head and squashed its brain,
And all the blood went down the drain.

Bill just smiled; he thought it was fine,
He munched on the cat till dinnertime.
Mum said we couldn't keep Bill any more,
But we might get a nicer dog from the store.

T is for tinea, between your toes, It's itchy as heck and it's bad on the nose.

55 There once was a girl named Keira,
Who drove any car that was near her.
It was not good to do,
Cos she was only age two,
And the rules on that couldn't be clearer.

56 I'm totally freaked out!

Wrestling freaks me out because I can't tell what is real,
Slimy things freak me out because of how they feel.
Worms freak me out; I can't tell which end is which,
Dibber-dobbers freak me out because they like to snitch.

Escalators freak me out because I don't know where they go,
Bald people freak me out, why won't their hair grow?
The number twenty freaks me out because I think it should be two-ty,
Dancing freaks me out because I cannot shake my booty.

57 Not-so perfect matches

Peanut butter and showers,
Baths and hairdryers.
Scissors and running,
Flannel pyjamas and fires.

Big fingers and little noses,
Two left feet and a jig.
Sunshine, red hair, and freckles,
A bald head and a really bad wig.

Crocodiles and chickens,
Tone deafness and singing.
Earwax and your tongue,
Your favourite show and the telephone ringing.

U is for umbrella, which isn't gross at all, I just think they're handy if rain starts to fall.

58 There once was a girl named Kelly,
Who spent three days watching the telly.
She watched some cool shows,
But was a bit on the nose,
Three days with no shower makes you smelly.

59 I used to think

I used to think my brother was cool,
Until one day he snubbed me at school.
I used to think that farts were funny,
Until one day one came out runny.

I used to think that dogs were cute,
Until one chewed my favourite boot.
I used to think vegetables weren't worthy,
Until we did a lesson on scurvy.

I used to think nose picking was okay,
Until I made my nose bleed one day.
I used to think Brussels sprouts tasted the worst,
And I still do! In fact, I think Brussels sprouts are cursed!

60 Animal advice

If you pull an elephant's tail it'll sit on you;
If you pull a crocodile's tail you'll be dead.
If you pull a skunk's tail it'll come right off;
If you pull a lion's tail it will bite off your head.

If you cuddle a bear you'll receive a bear hug;
If you cuddle a gorilla you'll be crushed.
If you cuddle an ant you'll need tiny little arms;
If you cuddle a cobra, that cuddle should be rushed.

V is for vomit, there's no way to spin it, It's gross how it always has bits of carrot in it.

61 There once was a man named John Pell,
Who just couldn't stand his wife's smell.
So he chopped off her head,
But she still wasn't dead,
So he chopped off her body as well.

62 The changing machine

I invented a changing machine – it was great!
But I went too far, and realised too late.
I changed my school marks to an A just like that,
And my stupid, ugly sister is now a stupid, ugly rat.

When my brother called my awesome action figure a doll,
I changed him into a toilet bowl.
I changed my cat into a lion, a fire-breathing one,
I changed my vegetables to ice-cream, oh man this was fun!

I was out of control, but I wanted to rule,
So I changed my hair into snakes, this was so cool.
But the snakes were cobras, and they bit me on the head,
And then I couldn't change the fact that I was dead.

63 People

Some people are tall, they tower up high,
It seems their heads might touch the sky.
Some people are short, little and squat,
They look up people's noses and see all the snot.

Some people have big feet, long with big toes,
Others have small feet but quite a big nose.
There are long legs and short legs, hairy and neat,
But they all go from the hips right down to the feet.

People with hands, and people with hooks,
So many sizes, so many looks.
But that doesn't matter, not in the end,
Not when it comes to you and your friends.

W is for white, the colour of zits, When you get a big pussy one it is just the pits.

64 There was a man named Mr Rouse,
Who fell down the stairs at his house.
The open mouth that he had,
Was very, very, bad,
Because he landed mouth-first on a mouse.

65 A fish

Once upon a time, a fish thought of a poem,
So he sat down to write it one night.
Unfortunately, his three-second memory,
Meant he forgot what he was going to write.

66 More opposites

If you play in mud you'll be dirty, if you have a shower you'll be clean,
If your mum's nice you won't be in trouble, but you will be if she's mean.
Silk is nice and smooth, but sandpaper is rough,
Wusses are little weaklings, and big tough guys are tough.

Angels are good, but bank robbers are bad,
My team winning makes me happy; my team losing makes me sad.
Giants are tall, but babies are short,
Don't drop the ball; catch it so it's caught.

Curves are curvy, and straights are straight,
When you're sick you throw up, but when you're
better you feel great!
Elephants are heavy, and mice are light,
My jumper is loose, but my jeans are tight.

X is for xylophone, a musical thing, Only made gross if I play one and sing.

67 If you're out collecting coconuts,
And you see any cannibal huts,
At dinner that night,
You should exit, stage right,
Or they'll spend the night eating your guts.

68 Pets

Don't get a dinosaur; they're not even real,
If you like to stroke your pet, don't get an electric eel.
Don't get a giraffe – that thought should be quashed,
Don't get a hippo because you might get squashed.

Don't get a bug because, well, it's a bug,
If you hate slimy things, you shouldn't get a slug.
Don't get a shark because no fishbowl's that big,
Don't get a pig because they eat like a pig.

Don't get a chameleon, you'd never, ever find it,
Don't get a tiger – if you went away who'd mind it?
Don't get a crocodile, that's obvious I think,
And don't get a skunk because they really, really stink.

69 The Rules

Don't swim after a meal, you must wait half an hour,
And before you go in the pool you should take a shower.
Don't run with scissors, and don't run at the pool,
Don't run in the corridors when you are at school.

Don't spend hours on the computer, but don't play in the sun;
Don't act too smart, but also don't play dumb.
Don't burp in public; don't fart at all,
And if you're playing inside, don't play with a ball.

Don't litter, don't swear, don't wear a hat inside,
Don't always use 'eenie, meenie, miney, moe' to decide.
There are plenty more rules to share, but I just don't have time,
If you follow these for starters, I think you should be fine.

Y is for yuck, which is what you'll shout out, When you are forced to eat yet another Brussels sprout.
Z is for z, the last letter we'll do, I hope this poem wasn't too gross for you.

70 If you think that you are pretty ace,
And you go to a crocodile's place.
You'd better step light,
'Cause if he gets a fright,
There's a good chance he'll chew off your face.

71 Changing the sheets

My bed's pretty gross because, I fear,
I changed the sheets only once last year.
The pillows have gone a weird kind of grey,
And there's been half a cake in there since May.
There's dirt, there are dust mites, and something
that goes 'squeak',
Oh, well, maybe I'll put on some clean sheets next week.

Horrifying Humour

1 Doctor, Doctor, I think I've been bitten by a vampire.
Drink this glass of water.
Will it make me better?
No, but I'll be able to see if your neck leaks!

2 Doctor, Doctor, I keep thinking I'm a vampire.
Necks, please!

3 Why aren't vampires welcome in blood banks?
Because they only make withdrawals.

4 Why was the young vampire a failure?
Because he fainted at the sight of blood.

5 Why did Dracula go to the dentist?
He had fang decay.

6 Where does Dracula wash?
In a bloodbath.

7 What's Dracula's car called?
A mobile blood unit.

8 Did you hear about the vampire who got taken away in a straightjacket?
He went batty.

9 What do vampires cross the sea in?
Blood vessels.

10 What is the vampire's favourite slogan?
Please Give Blood Generously.

11 Why did Dracula take some medicine?
To stop his coffin.

12 Where does Dracula go fishing?
In a bloodstream.

13 Why is Count Dracula skinny?
Because he eats necks to nothing.

14 Person 1: *'Why are you wearing garlic around your neck?'*
Person 2: *'It keeps away vampires.'*
Person 1: *'But there aren't any vampires.'*
Person 2: *'See, it works.'*

15 What is Dracula's favourite fruit?
Necktarines!

16 What is Dracula's favourite ice-cream flavour?
Vein-illa!

17 What do vampires have for a snack?
Blood oranges.

18 What does a vampire never order at a restaurant?
Stake.

19 How does Dracula eat his food?
In bite-sized pieces.

20 Where does Dracula go swimming?
In a pool of blood.

21 Why was Dracula confused at the dinner party?
Because the guests were all blue bloods.

22 What is a baby vampire called?
A suckling.

23 What does a vampire say in court?
I swear to tell the tooth, the whole tooth, and nothing but the tooth.

24 Why wouldn't the vampire eat his soup?
It clotted.

25 Mother vampire to son: 'Hurry up and eat your breakfast before it turns into a scab.'

26 What's a vampire's favourite kind of coffee?
De-coffin-ated!

27 First vampire: *'I don't think much of your sister's neck!'*
Second vampire: *'Don't worry, just eat the vegetables.'*

28 Why did the vampire go to the orthodontist?
To improve his bite.

29 What do you call a single vampire?
A bat-chelor.

30 What did the vampire say when he had bitten someone?
'It's been nice gnawing you!'

31 Why don't people kiss vampires?
Because they have bat breath.

32 Did you hear about the vampire who died of a broken heart?
She had loved in vein.

33 Why is the vampire so unpopular?
Because he is a pain in the neck.

34 What did the witch say to the vampire?
'Get a life!'

35 What do you get when you cross a vampire with a computer?
Love at first byte.

36 What happened at the vampires' reunion?
All the blood relations went.

37 What do you call an old and foolish vampire?
A silly old sucker.

38 Who is a vampire likely to fall in love with?
The girl necks door.

39 What do you do if you're surrounded by a witch, a werewolf, a vampire and two ghosts?
Hope you're at a costume party.

40 What job does Dracula have with the Transylvanian baseball team?
He's the bat boy.

41 What did they call Dracula when he refereed the World Series?
The Vumpire.

42 What would you get if you cross a teacher with a vampire?
Lots of blood tests.

43 Who won the race between Count Dracula and Countess Dracula?
It was neck and neck.

44 If a wizard were knocked out by Dracula in a fight, what would he be?
Out for the Count.

45 Why did the young vampire follow his dad's profession?
Because it was in his blood.

46 What is the first thing vampires learn at school?
The alphabat.

47 Why is Hollywood full of vampires?
They need someone to play the bit parts.

48 Why did the vampire give up acting?
He couldn't find a part he could sink his teeth into.

49 Did you hear about the vampire comedian?
He specialised in biting satire.

50 Why do vampires play poker?
Because they like playing for high stakes.

51 What do you get if you cross a dinosaur with a vampire?
A blood shortage.

52 How many vampires does it take to change a light bulb?
None. They love the dark.

53 What do you get when you cross a vampire and a snowman?
Frostbite!

54 What do you get when you cross a vampire with a dwarf?
A monster that sucks blood out of people's kneecaps.

55 What is Dracula's favourite song?
Fang-ks for the Memories.

56 How do monsters like their eggs?
Terrifried.

57 What's a vampire's favourite dance?
The fangdango.

58 What is a vampire's favourite sport?
Batminton.

59 What's a vampire's favourite animal?
A giraffe.

60 What's a vampire's favourite dog?
A bloodhound!

61 What do you think the tiniest vampire gets up to at night?
Your ankles.

62 What is Dracula's favourite place in New York?
The Vampire State Building!

63 How does Dracula look when he goes out at night?
Fang-tastic.

64 What did the vampire do to stop his son biting his nails?
He cut all his fingers off.

65 What do Hungarian monsters eat?
Ghoulash.

66 Why did the monster eat the North Pole?
He was in the mood for a frozen dinner.

67 What do sea monsters eat?
Fish and ships.

68 What did the sea monster say when it saw the brand-new cruise ship sail past?
'Yum. Launch time.'

69 Does a monster need a menu while vacationing on a cruise ship?
No, just the passenger list.

70 What do you call a monster sleeping in a chandelier?
A light sleeper.

71 What kind of cheese do monsters eat?
Monsterella!

72 What do monsters have mid-morning?
A coffin break.

73 What did the monster say when he saw a rush-hour train full of passengers?
Great! A chew-chew train.

74 Little Monster: *'Should I eat my fries with my fingers?'*
Mum Monster: *'No, you should eat them separately!'*

75 Little Monster: 'I hate my teacher's guts!'
Mum Monster: 'Then just eat around them!'

76 What do you do with a blue monster?
Try to cheer him up a bit.

77 What happened to the monster that took the five o'clock train home?
He had to give it back.

78 What should you take if a monster invites you to dinner?
Someone who can't run as fast as you.

79 What did the monster want to eat in the restaurant?
The finger bowl.

80 What does a monster mummy say to her kids at dinnertime?
Don't speak with someone in your mouth.

81 Why was the monster catching centipedes?
He wanted scrambled legs for breakfast.

82 Why did the monster buy an axe?
Because he wanted to get ahead in life.

83 What does a monster say when introduced?
Pleased to eat you.

84 What happened when the ice monster ate a spicy salsa?
He blew his cool.

85 Did you hear what happened to Ray when he met the man-eating monster?
He became an ex-Ray.

86 What does a monster eat after he's been to the dentist?
The dentist.

87 How did the monster cure his sore throat?
By gargoyling every day.

88 Why did the monster eat his music teacher?
Because his Bach was worse than his bite.

89 On which day do monsters eat people?
Chewsday.

90 Who is the best dancer at a monster party?
The Boogie Man!

91 What does a boy monster do when a girl monster rolls her eyes at him?
He rolls them back to her.

92 How do you greet a three-headed monster?
'Hello, hello, hello.'

93 Why are Cyclops couples happy together?
Because they always see eye to eye.

94 Did you hear about the girl monster who wasn't pretty and wasn't ugly?
She was pretty ugly.

95 Did you hear about the monster who sent his picture to a lonely hearts club?
They sent it back, saying they weren't that lonely.

96 Why did the monster eat the light bulb?
He wanted some light refreshment.

97 Who did the monster take to the Halloween dance?
His ghoul friend.

98 What do young female monsters do at parties?
They go around looking for edible bachelors.

99 What aftershave do monsters prefer?
Brute.

100 What do you think when you see a monster?
I hope he hasn't seen me.

101 Why did the monster paint himself in rainbow-coloured stripes?
He wanted to hide in a crayon box.

102 What do you call a good-looking, kind and considerate monster?
A complete failure.

103 What monster is the most untidy?
The Loch Mess monster.

104 What did the Loch Ness monster say to his friend?
Long time no sea.

105 What did Frankenstein's monster do when he saw the monster catcher approaching?
He bolted.

106 How does Frankenstein's monster eat?
He bolts his food down.

107 What did Frankenstein's monster say when he was struck by lightning?
Thanks, I needed that.

108 Why did it take the monster ten months to finish a book?
Because he wasn't very hungry.

109 What do you call a monster that comes to collect your laundry?
An undie-taker.

110 How does Frankenstein's monster sit in his chair?
Bolt upright.

111 Where do monsters send their clothes for cleaning?
The dry screamers.

112 What do you call a sleeping monster who won't stay quiet?
Frankensnore.

113 What happened to Frankenstein's monster when he was caught speeding?
He was fined $50 and dismantled for six months.

114 What do you call the winner of a monster beauty contest?
Ugly.

115 What do you get when you cross a skunk with Frankenstein?
Stinkenstein!

116 How many monsters would it take to fill up your classroom?
I don't know. I wouldn't hang around to find out.

117 What's the name of a clever monster?
Frank Einstein.

118 What's a monster's favourite shape?
A vicious circle.

119 Why did the young monster take a runner to school in his lunch?
Because he liked fast food.

120 The mother monster asked her son what he was doing with a saw, and if he'd seen his brother.
'You mean my new half-brother, Mum,' he replied.

121 What do you call a 20-tonne two-headed monster?
Sir.

122 What time is it when a monster gets into your bed?
Time to get a new bed!

123 Why did the little monsters stay up all night?
They were studying for a blood test.

124 What's a good job for a young monster?
Chop assistant.

125 What would you get if you cross a teacher with a vampire?
Lots of blood tests.

126 How does a monster count to 13?
On his fingers.

127 How do man-eating monsters count to a thousand?
On their warts.

128 Why was the big, hairy, two-headed monster top of the school class?
Because two heads are better than one.

129 What did the shy pebble monster say?
I wish I was a little boulder.

130 What do you call a ten-foot-tall monster?
Shorty.

131 Why did the young monster knit herself three socks?
She grew another foot.

132 Did you hear about the monster who had eight arms?
He said they came in handy.

133 What does a monster call his parents?
Dead and mummy.

134 What do you call a three-metre-long, two-headed monster?
Anything it wants.

135 Why should you never touch a monster's tail?
It's the end of the monster and the end of you.

136 What do you do with a green monster?
Put him in a paper bag till he ripens.

137 What type of horses do monsters ride?
Night mares.

138 What is big, hairy and bounces up and down?
A monster on a pogo stick.

139 Why isn't the Abominable Snowman scared of people?
Because he doesn't believe in them.

140 What happened when the Abominable Snowman ate hot pepper?
He melted.

141 What do you call a monster that was locked in the freezer overnight?
A cool ghoul.

142 What did the angry monster do when he got his gas bill?
He exploded.

143 How does a yeti feel when it gets a cold?
Abominable.

144 What is white, lives in the Himalayas and lays eggs?
The Abominable Snow Chicken.

145 If you crossed the Loch Ness monster with a shark, what would you get?
Loch Jaws.

146 What should you do if a monster runs through your front door?
Run out the back door.

147 What do you call a monster airline steward?
A fright attendant.

148 How do you know when there's a monster under your bed?
Your nose touches the ceiling.

149 What is the first thing a monster does when you give him an axe?
Make out a chopping list.

150 What story do little witches like to hear at bedtime?
Ghoul deluxe and the three scares.

151 What kind of tests do witch teachers give?
Hex-aminations.

152 What happened to the naughty school witch?
She was ex-spelled.

153 What do you call two witches that share a room?
Broom mates.

154 What is a witch's favourite class in school?
Spelling.

155 What did the witch say to the ugly toad?
I'd put a curse on you – but somebody beat me to it.

156 What do you call a pretty and friendly witch?
A failure.

157 Why do witches fly on broomsticks?
Because it's better than walking.

158 What did the skeleton say to the twin witches?
Which witch is which?

159 What did the wizard say to his witch girlfriend?
Hello, gore-juice.

160 What happened when the young wizard met the young witch?
It was love at first fright.

161 What happened when the baby witch was born?
It was so ugly its parents ran away from home.

162 First witch: *'My, hasn't your little girl grown!'*
Second witch: *'Yes, she's certainly gruesome.'*

163 What do you call a witch that lives at the beach?
A sand witch!

164 Why do witches have stiff joints?
They get broomatism.

165 Who did the witch call when her broom was stolen?
The flying squad.

166 Why did the witch put her broom in the washing machine?
She wanted a clean sweep.

167 Why do witches get good bargains?
Because they're good at haggling.

168 What do you call a nervous witch?
A twitch.

169 What feature do witches love on their computer?
The spell-checker.

170 What do you call a witch without a broomstick?
A witch-hiker.

171 How many witches does it take to change a light bulb?
Just one, but she changes it into a toad.

172 Why did the witches go on strike?
Because they wanted sweeping reforms.

173 Did you hear about the weather wizard?
He's forecasting sunny spells.

174 Why couldn't the witch race her horse in the Witches' Derby?
Because it was having a spell.

175 What is a witch's favourite movie?
Broom with a View.

176 How do you make a witch itch? *Take away the W.*

177 Which of the witch's friends eats the fastest?
The goblin.

178 What do witches put in their hair?
Scare spray.

179 What do you get when you cross a heater with a witch?
A hot spell.

180 How does a witch tell the time?
With a witch watch!

181 What vehicles race at the Witches' Formula One Grand Prix?
Vroomsticks.

182 What do you get when you cross a witch and a skunk?
An ugly smell.

183 What noise does a witch's breakfast cereal make?
Snap, cackle and pop!

184 What happened when the old witch went to see a wicked film?
The manager told her to cut the cackle.

185 What do you call a motorcycle belonging to a witch?
A brooooooooom stick!

186 How does a witch make scrambled eggs?
She holds the pan and gets two friends to make the stove shake with fright.

187 What do you get if you cross a ghost with a packet of chips?
Snacks that go crunch in the night.

188 What is the favourite fair ride for little ghosts?
The roller-ghoster.

189 What does a ghost have to get before he can scare anyone?
A haunting licence.

190 What game do young ghosts love?
Hide and shriek.

191 How can you tell what a ghost is getting for its birthday?
By feeling its presence.

192 Why do ghosts like the Spice Girls?
Because they're an all-ghoul band.

193 A ghost walks into a bar.
Bartender: 'Sorry, we don't serve spirits here.'

194 Why do ghosts go to parties?
To have a wail of a time.

195 Did you hear about the ghost who ate all the Christmas decorations?
He got tinselitis.

196 Did you hear about the ghosts' race?
It was a dead heat.

197 Where do ghosts play golf?
At the golf corpse.

198 What should you say when you meet a ghost?
How do you boo, sir?

199 What did the ghost buy for his wife?
A see-through nightie.

200 Where do Australian ghosts live?
In the Northern Terror-tory.

201 What do ghosts eat for dinner?
Spook-etti.

202 What does a ghost do when he gets in a car?
Puts his sheet belt on!

203 What is a ghost's favourite dessert?
Boo-berries and I Scream!

204 What do you get when a ghost sits in a tree?
Petrified wood!

205 When do ghosts usually appear?
Just before someone screams.

206 Why do ghosts hate rain?
It dampens their spirits.

207 Why are ghosts always tired?
Because they are dead on their feet.

208 Why don't ghosts bother telling lies?
Because you can see right through them.

209 Why didn't the ghost eat liver?
He didn't have the stomach for it!

210 What do you call a ghost's mum and dad?
Transparents.

211 Where do baby ghosts go during the day?
The day scare centre!

212 Which monster is the best soccer player?
The ghoul keeper.

213 What trees do ghosts like best?
Ceme-trees.

214 Did you hear about the musical ghost?
He wrote haunting melodies.

215 What did one ghost say to the other?
Don't spook until you're spooken to.

216 Which ghost is President of France?
Charles de Ghoul.

217 What is a ghost's favourite bedtime story?
Little Boo Peep!

218 What song did the band play at the Demons and Ghouls ball?
'Demons are a Ghoul's Best Friend.'

219 Which ghost can always get out of a tight situation?
Whoooo-dini.

220 What is a ghost's favourite book?
A whooo-dunnit.

221 Why can ghosts speak Latin?
Because it's a dead language.

222 What do you get when you cross a police officer with a ghost?
An inspectre.

223 What do ghosts use to type letters?
A type-frighter.

224 What do you get if you cross Bambi with a ghost?
Bamboo.

225 What kind of mistake does a ghost make?
A boo-boo!

226 What does a ghost read every day?
His horrorscope.

227 What do little zombies play?
Corpse and robbers.

228 Why do they have a fence around the graveyard?
Everyone is dying to get in!

229 Why did the zombie decide to stay in his coffin?
He felt rotten.

230 Do zombies have trouble getting dates?
No, they can usually dig someone up.

231 Do zombies like the dark?
Of corpse they do.

232 What don't zombies wear on boat trips?
Life jackets.

233 How can you tell if a corpse is angry?
It flips its lid.

234 What did the zombie get his medal for?
Deadication.

235 What type of music do zombies like best?
Soul music.

236 Why are graveyards so noisy?
Because of all the coffin!

237 What did the baby zombie want for his birthday?
A deady bear.

238 What do you get if you cross a zombie with a boy scout?
A creature that scares old ladies across the street.

239 What do you call a detective skeleton?
Sherlock Bones.

240 Why couldn't the skeleton go to the dance?
He had no body to go with.

241 Why do skeletons play the piano in church?
Because they don't have any organs.

242 Why didn't the skeleton want to go to work?
Because his heart wasn't in it.

243 What happened when the gravediggers went on strike?
Their job was done by a skeleton crew.

244 How does a skeleton call his friends?
On a telebone.

245 Where do skeletons go swimming?
In the Dead Sea.

246 How do you make a skeleton laugh?
Tickle his funnybone.

247 What's a skeleton's favourite musical instrument?
A trom-bone.

248 What do you call a skeleton who sits around doing nothing?
Lazy bones.

249 Why are skeletons usually so calm?
Nothing gets under their skin.

250 Where do skeletons keep their money?
In a joint account.

251 Where do you find a skeleton's address?
In the bone book.

252 What kind of street does a monster like?
A dead end.

253 Why do skeletons hate winter?
Because the cold goes right to their bones.

254 What did one skeleton say to the other?
If we had any guts, we'd get out of here.

255 Mum, everyone at school calls me a werewolf.
Ignore them and comb your face.

256 What's a skeleton?
Someone with their outsides off and their insides out.

257 Why don't skeletons wear shorts?
Because they have bony knees.

258 What do you call a dumb skeleton?
A numbskull.

259 Why do skeletons drink milk?
Because it's good for the bones.

260 Why are skeletons afraid of dogs?
Because dogs like bones.

261 Why didn't the skeleton bother to defend itself in court?
Because it didn't have a leg to stand on.

262 What kind of plate does a skeleton eat off?
Bone china.

263 Why didn't the skeleton cross the road?
Because he didn't have the guts!

264 Two cannibals were having lunch.
'Your girlfriend makes a great soup,' said one to the other.
'Yes!' agreed the first. *'But I'm going to miss her!'*

265 Why don't cannibals eat weather forecasters?
Because they give them wind.

266 What did the cannibal say when he was full?
'I couldn't eat another mortal.'

267 Where do cannibals work?
At head office.

268 First Cannibal: *'My girlfriend's a tough old bird.'*
Second Cannibal: *'You should have left her in the oven for another half hour.'*

269 How can you help a hungry cannibal?
Give him a hand.

270 What did the cannibal have for breakfast?
Baked beings.

271 What is a cannibal's favourite soup?
One with a lot of body.

272 What's the favourite game at a cannibal's birthday party?
Swallow the leader.

273 What do the guests do at a cannibal wedding?
Toast the bride and groom.

274 Why did the cannibal kidnap the tourist?
He wanted takeaway food.

275 First Cannibal: *'Who was that girl I saw you with last night?'*
Second Cannibal: *'That was no girl, that was my dinner.'*

276 Why did the cannibal live on his own?
He'd had his fill of other people.

277 Mummy, Mummy, when are we going to have Grandma for dinner?
We haven't finished eating your father yet.

278 Daddy, can I have another glass of water, please?
Okay, but that's the twelfth one you've had tonight.
Yes I know, but my bedroom is still on fire.

279 Mummy, Mummy, Daddy's on fire.
Quick! Go get the marshmallows!

280 Mummy, Mummy, why can't we give Grandma a proper burial?
Oh, just keep flushing.

281 Mummy, Mummy, why do I keep going round in circles?
Be quiet or I'll nail your other foot to the floor.

282 Mummy, Mummy, can I play with Rover?
We've already dug him up three times this week.

283 Mummy, Mummy, Daddy just put Rover down.
I'm sure he had a good reason for it.
But he promised I could do it.

284 Mummy, Mummy, my head hurts.
Then don't stand in front of the dartboard.

285 Mummy, Mummy, are you sure you bake bread this way?
Just get back in. I can't close the oven door.

286 Mummy, Mummy, I just chopped off my foot.
Then hop out of the kitchen. I just mopped the floor.

287 Mummy, Mummy, I think I have a split personality.
Then clean up your brother's room too.

288 Mummy, Mummy, Daddy's hammering on the roof again.
I'll just drive a little faster.

289 *How to Keep Out a Vampire* by Dora Steele

290 *The Long Sleep* by Anna Sthetic

291 *The Greediest Monster* by Buster Gutt

292 *Falling from a Height* by Eileen Toofar

293 *In the Cannibal's Cauldron* by Mandy Ceased

294 *Foaming at the Mouth* by Dee Monic

295 *Egyptian Mummies* by M Barmer

296 *A Ghost in the Attic* by Howie Wales

297 *Ghosts and Ghouls* by Sue Pernatural

298 *The Omen* by B Warned

299 *A Terrible Nightmare* by Gladys Over

300 *Famous Frights* by Terry Fied

301 *The Poltergeist* by Eve L Spirit

302 *My Crystal Ball* by CA Lot

IRRESISTIBLE
INSULTS

1 You are so ugly the only dates you get are on a calendar.

2 Either you're very ugly or your neck has stepped in something.

3 Everyone has the right to be ugly, but you abused the privilege.

4 You are so ugly they didn't give you a costume when you auditioned for Star Wars.

5 You are so ugly, when you walk into a bank they turn off the surveillance cameras.

6 You're dark and handsome. When it's dark, you're handsome.

7 You are so ugly, when you enter a room the mice jump on chairs.

8 You are so ugly they push your face into dough to make cookies.

9 'Daddy, Daddy, there's a monster at the door with a really ugly face.'
'Tell him you've already got one!'

10 If I were as ugly as you I'd wear a mask.

11 'Do you think that I'll lose my looks when I get older?'
'With luck, yes.'

12 Boy: 'You've got a face like a million dollars.'
Girl: *'Have I really?'*
Boy: 'Sure, it's green and wrinkly!'

13 You are so ugly, when you went on a package tour to where headhunters live you were the only survivor.

14 'My husband always carries my photo in his pocket. It once saved his life when a mugger tried to stab him.'
'Your face would stop anything.'

15 You are so ugly, when you were born your mother said, 'What a treasure!' and your father said, 'Yes, let's go bury it.'

16 Turn the other cheek. On second thoughts, don't. The view is just as ugly on that side.

17 Don't you need a licence to be that ugly?

18 'I've just come back from the beauty salon.'
'What a pity it was closed.'

19 You're so ugly, when a wasp stings you it has to shut its eyes!

20 You are so ugly, when you stand on the beach the tide won't come in.

21 You are so ugly, when you try to take a bath the water jumps out!

22 You are so ugly you could turn Medusa to stone!

23 I hear you were the last one born in your family. I can understand that. You're enough to discourage anyone.

24 You are so ugly you made an onion cry.

25 You are so ugly even Rice Bubbles won't talk to you!

26 Last time I saw someone as ugly as you I had to pay admission.

27 Woman: *'When I'm old and ugly, will you still love me?'*
Man: *'I do, don't I?'*

28 'Shall I put the TV on?'
'Well, it would certainly improve the view in here.'

29 You are so ugly you have to trick or treat over the phone.

30 'Boys fall in love with me at first sight.'
'I bet they change their minds when they look again.'

31 You are so ugly people go as you to Halloween parties.

32 Don't look out of the window. People will think that it's Halloween.

33 You are so ugly, when you joined an ugly contest they said, 'Sorry, no professionals allowed.'

34 You are not as stupid as you look. That would be impossible.

35 'I've kept my youthful complexion.'
'So I see, all spotty.'

36 Your face is so ugly it would make a train take a dirt road.

37 'What would it take to make me look good?'
'A lot of distance between you and me.'

38 Your dad is so dumb he walked into the electricity company with a $20 note in each ear because he received a bill saying he was $40 in arrears.

39 Your sister is so ugly she was asked to remove her mask at a masked ball – and she wasn't wearing one.

40 Your brother is so dumb, when he swam across the English Channel he got tired halfway and swam back.

41 Your dad is so dumb, when he locked his keys in the car he called a mechanic to get the family out.

42 Your mum is so ugly your father takes her to work with him so that he doesn't have to kiss her goodbye.

43 Your dad is so hairy they filmed *Gorillas in the Mist* in his shower.

44 You are so ugly, when you were a baby your mum had to feed you with a slingshot.

45 Your granddad is so dumb he got locked in a supermarket overnight and died of starvation.

46 My cousin spent heaps on deodorant, until he found out people just didn't like him . . .

47 Your mum is so dumb, when she fills in forms that say 'Sign Here', she writes 'Taurus'.

48 Your mum is so dumb she put lipstick on her forehead because she wanted to make up her mind.

49 You are so ugly, when you were born the doctor turned you over and said, 'Look. Twins.'

50 Your sister has everything a man desires – bulging muscles and a moustache.

51 If I had a brother like you, I'd put myself up for adoption.

52 What's small, annoying and really ugly?
I don't know but it comes when I call my sister's name.

53 'My sister went on a crash diet.'
'Is that why she looks a wreck?'

54 I haven't spoken to my sister for over a year. I don't like to interrupt her.

55 Some women are blonde on their mother's side, some from their father's side – your mum is from Peroxide.

56 Your dad is so dumb he locked himself in a motorbike.

57 You are so careless, when you tried to fit a new window you broke it with a hammer.

58 Your family is so poor, when the doorbell rings your sister has to shout out, 'Ding, Dong.'

59 Your mum is so clumsy, when she fell in love, she broke it.

60 Your granddad is so old he can whistle and clean his teeth at the same time.

61 My dad once stopped a man ill-treating a donkey.
It was a case of brotherly love. . .

62 Your mum is so ugly she went to a beauty salon and it took three hours . . . for an estimate.

63 Your dad is so dumb he only gets a half-hour lunch break because if he took any longer he would have to be retrained.

64 You will never be the man your mother is.

65 A man came running out of his house as the garbage truck was driving by.
Man: *'Did I miss the garbage collection?'*
Garbage man: *'No, jump in.'*

66 Your breath is so bad that people look forward to your farts.

67 'Is that a new perfume I smell?'
'It is, and you do.'

68 Your feet are so smelly, your shoes refuse to come out of the closet.

69 'What smells worse than a bad egg?'
'You do!'

70 'You smell funny.'
'That's my soap. I don't suppose you've smelt it before.'

71 'How do you find my breath?'
'Offensive, it's keeping you alive.'

72 You don't need to use an insult, you could just use your breath.

73 'We should try and fight air pollution.'
'You could start by stopping breathing.'

74 Waiter, do you serve crabs in this restaurant?
Yes sir, we serve anyone.

75 I've heard you're the big noise around here. I think you should cut back on the baked beans.

76 Your teeth are so yellow that your eyes light up when you close your mouth.

77 You might not know much but you lead the league in nostril hair.

78 'Why are you bathing in such dirty water?'
'It wasn't dirty when I got in.'

79 If it's true that opposites attract, you'll meet someone who is good-looking, intelligent and cultured.

80 I like you a lot. But then, I've never had good taste.

81 That isn't your forehead, it's your hair trying to run away from your face.

82 'People like that don't grow on trees you know.'
'No, they normally swing under them.'

83 My sister has such a sharp tongue we don't need a knife to carve the Sunday roast.

84 Is that your face or did your neck throw up?

85 Go and sit down. Nobody can stand you.

86 You are so slow you can't even catch your breath.

87 You're so lazy, that if you woke up with nothing to do, you'd go to bed with it only half done.

88 'You'd make a good exchange student.'
'Do you think so?'
'Yes, we might be able to exchange you for someone nice.'

89 Someone told me you are not fit to live with pigs but I stuck up for you and said you were.

90 You know I do understand you. I seem to have a way with dumb animals.

91 When I want your opinion I'll rattle your cage.

92 You are so ugly your mum had to tie a steak around your neck to get the dog to play with you.

93 You are a monument to the human race. And you know what pigeons do to monuments.

94 'Did you hear that he was buried face down?'
'Why?'
'So he could see where he was going.'

95 'Can you cure my fleas?'
'Maybe, what's wrong with them?'

96 His death won't be listed under 'Obituaries', more like 'Neighbourhood Improvements'.

97 What's the difference between you and a wild camel?
One is a big, smelly, bad-tempered beast and the other is an animal.

98 You are so short and hairy, when you walk around the house your mother screams, 'Mouse!'

99 Your dog is so slow he brings in last week's newspaper.

100 May a thousand fleas from a camel's back infest your armpit and keep you warm at night.

101 A man walks into a restaurant with a skunk under his arm.
Waiter: *'You can't bring that smelly thing in here.'*
Skunk: *'Sorry. I'll leave him outside.'*

102 First Man: *'My girlfriend eats like a bird.'*
Second Man: *'You mean she hardly eats a thing?'*
First Man: *'No, she eats slugs and worms.'*

103 You are so dumb you threw the butter out of the window because you wanted to see a butterfly.

104 I thought of you all day today. I was at the zoo.

105 You remind me of the southern most portion of a northern bound horse.

106 How did you get here? Did someone leave your cage open?

107 If I throw a stick, will you go away?

108 They call him 'Rope' because he is always stringing people along.

109 You are so scared you wear a life jacket when you sleep on a waterbed.

110 You remind me of a calendar. Your days are numbered.

111 I could make a monkey out of you, but why should I take all the credit?

112 I don't consider you a vulture. I consider you something a vulture would eat.

113 You have the face of a saint. A Saint Bernard, that is.

114 I'm looking forward to the pleasure of your company since I haven't had it yet.

115 I hear you were born on a farm. Any more in the litter?

116 Doctor, Doctor, I have a hoarse throat.
The resemblance doesn't end there.

117 You are so dumb you put a chicken in a hot bath so it would lay hard-boiled eggs.

118 You are so dumb it takes you an hour to cook one-minute noodles.

119 A woman woke her husband in the middle of the night.
'There's a burglar in the kitchen eating the cake I made this morning!' she said.
'Who should I call?' asked her husband. 'The police or an ambulance?'

120 'Do you like my cottage pie?'
'Umm, next time try taking the drains out first.'

121 What are you going to do for a face when the monkey wants his butt back?

122 'This food isn't fit for a pig.'
'I'll get some for you that is then.'

123 You are so dumb you fed money to your cow because you wanted to get rich milk.

124 'Waiter, I'd like burnt steak and soggy chips with a grimy, bitter salad.'
'I'm afraid the chef won't cook that for you, sir.'
'He did yesterday.'

125 You are such a bad cook even the maggots get takeaway.

126 'I love biscuits.'
'That's because you're crackers.'

127 'I don't like soup.'
'I expect you can't get it to stay on the fork, can you?'

128 You are so slow you have to speed up to stop!

129 You are so dumb you stared at the orange juice container because it said 'Concentrate'.

130 'I hear the team's prospects are looking up.'
'I didn't know you were leaving.'

131 Our new player is called 'Cinderella' because he keeps running away from the ball.

132 'I love golf. I could play like this forever.'
'Don't you want to improve?'

133 'I've never played so badly.'
'You mean you've actually played before?'

134 You are so dumb, when you went water-skiing you spent your whole holiday looking for a sloping lake.

135 'Coach, how was my dribbling on the court?'
'Terrible. Close your mouth.'

136 'What position do you play in the football team?'
'I'm not sure, though the coach calls me one of the drawbacks.'

137 'Coach, how would you have played that last shot?'
'In disguise.'

138 'Coach, how do I stand for a team trial?'
'You don't stand, you grovel.'

139 Our goalkeeper is so dumb he won't catch the ball because he thinks that's what the net is for.

140 You are so dumb you think a cartoon is something you sing in the car.

141 You are so dumb you fell in the sink while tap dancing.

142 'I can play piano by ear.'
'And I can fiddle with my toes.'

143 'This piece of music is haunting.'
'That's because you're murdering it.'

144 You're multi-talented. You do a hundred things badly.

145 'Do you find me entertaining?'
'You're too dim to entertain a thought.'

146 'Do you notice how my voice fills the hall?'
'Yes, and did you notice how many people left to make way for it?'

147 You are so dumb you take your bicycle to bed because you don't want to walk in your sleep.

148 You are so dumb, when you held up the music store you told them to give you the lute.

149 'What shall I sing next?'
'Do you know Bridge Over Troubled Waters?'
'Yes.'
'Then go and jump off it.'

150 He's good at everything he does. And as far as I can see he usually does nothing.

151 'Mrs Johnston, your daughter would be a fine dancer, except for two things.'
'What are they?'
'Both feet!'

152 You are so dumb you invented a chocolate teapot.

153 'My doctor says I should give up football.'
'So he's seen you play too then.'

154 There is no vaccine against stupidity.

155 When you were born the doctor slapped your mother.

156 You are so dumb you tiptoe past the medicine cabinet so that you don't wake the sleeping pills.

157 I heard you went to have your head examined but the doctors found nothing there.

158 Doctor, Doctor, everyone hates me.
Don't be stupid, not everyone has met you yet.

159 You are so dumb you jump up and down before taking medicine because the label reads 'Shake well before using'.

160 You're growing on me – like a wart.

161 I'm not saying my wife isn't good-looking but when she goes to the doctor he tells her to open her mouth and go 'Moooo'.

162 You are so dumb you can't pass a blood test.

163 You should go to a dentist and have some wisdom teeth put in.

164 If I ever need a brain transplant, I'd choose yours because I'd want a brain that had never been used.

165 You are so dumb you got seventeen of your friends to accompany you to the movies because you heard it was not for under-18s.

166 I would never enter into a battle of wits with an unarmed person.

167 You are as sharp as a bowling ball.

168 'Do you know what nice people do at the weekend?'
'No.'
'I didn't think you would.'

169 'I do lots of exercise.'
'I thought so. That's why you're so long-winded.'

170 He is the kind of a man that you would use as a blueprint to build an idiot.

171 You're so unpopular even your answering machine hangs up on you.

172 If what you don't know can't hurt you, you'll live forever.

173 Keep talking, someday you'll say something intelligent.

174 You are so boring you won't even talk to yourself.

175 They say that truth is stranger than fiction. And you are the proof.

176 You are so dumb it takes you three hours to watch 'Sixty Minutes'.

177 You are a few clowns short of a circus.

178 'Haven't I seen you on TV?'
'Well yes, I do appear off and on. How do you like me?'
'Off.'

179 You are so dumb you push when playing tug of war.

180 You have an open mind. Ideas just slip straight out.

181 'I've changed my mind.'
'Great, does the new one work any better?'

182 I bet your brain feels as good as new, seeing that you've never used it.

183 The closest you'll ever come to a brain storm is a light drizzle.

184 'How long can someone live without a brain?'
'How old are you?'

185 You're so dumb, when you went to the mind reader they couldn't find anything to read.

186 Just because you have a sharp tongue does not mean you have a keen mind.

187 Brains aren't everything. In fact, in your case they're nothing.

188 I know you are nobody's fool but maybe someone will adopt you.

189 You are so dumb, if you had a brain you'd take it out and play with it.

190 'How dare you tell everyone I'm stupid.'
'Sorry, I didn't realise it was a secret.'

191 Calling you stupid would be an insult to stupid people.

192 I don't know what makes you so stupid, but it really works!

193 You are as smart as bait.

194 You have a photographic mind. It's a pity it has never been developed.

195 You are so dumb you threw a rock at the ground, and missed.

196 There's no point in telling some people a joke with a double meaning.
They wouldn't understand either of them!

197 How do you make a stupid person laugh on a Thursday?
Tell him a joke on Monday.

198 How do you keep a nerd in suspense for 24 hours?
I'll tell you tomorrow.

199 Hold still, I'm trying to imagine you with a personality.

200 Don't let your mind wander – it's too little to be let out alone.

201 I don't think you are a fool. But then what's my opinion against thousands of others?

202 I'd like to leave you with one thought . . . but I'm not sure you have anywhere to put it!

203 It's perfectly all right to have an unexpressed thought. In fact, in your case I recommend it.

204 I'll try being nicer if you try being smarter.

205 You are the kind of friend a person can depend on. You're always around when you need me.

206 Statistics say that one in three people is wacky.
So check your friends and if two of them seem okay, you're the one . . .

207 Your house is so nasty I tripped over a rat and a cockroach stole my wallet.

208 If you were any dumber you'd have to be watered twice a week.

209 You forgot to pay your brain bill.

210 You are so dumb you burnt your ear because you were ironing when the phone rang.

211 You are so dumb you burnt your other ear when the caller rang back.

212 You are so dumb, when you heard 90% of all accidents occur around the home you moved.

213 You are a few peas short of a casserole.

214 You are so dumb you run around and around your bed so you can catch up with your sleep.

215 You are so dumb you refused to buy a ticket for the door prize because you already have a door.

216 You are so dumb you ate yeast and shoe polish for breakfast because you wanted to rise and shine in the morning.

217 You are so dumb you went round and round in a revolving door looking for the doorknob.

218 Your incompetence is an inspiration to morons everywhere.

219 I'd like to help you out. Which way did you come in?

220 You don't bore people with long speeches. You can bore them with a short speech.

221 Go ahead, tell us everything you know. It'll only take 10 seconds.

222 You are such a bad typist you type 60 mistakes a minute.

223 You are so dumb your computer has whiteout all over the screen.

224 People say you're a perfect idiot. I tell them you may not be perfect but you are doing a great job being an idiot.

225 You are so dumb you got fired from the banana factory for throwing out all the bent ones.

226 You are so dumb you fell out of a tree after you were told to rake up the leaves.

227 'How many people work in your office?'
'About half of them.'

228 They call him 'Caterpillar' because he has got where he is by crawling.

229 'I hear she is a business woman.'
'Yes, her nose is always in other people's business.'

230 Handsome Harry: *'Every time I walk past a girl, she sighs.'*
Wisecracking William: *'With relief!'*

231 'He has an answer for everything.'
'Yes, the wrong one.'

232 That dress fits you like a glove. It sticks out in five places.

233 You are so dumb you wore a wet shirt all day because the label said 'wash and wear'.

234 You are so dumb you invented an ejector seat on a helicopter.

235 You are so dumb you invented a parachute that opens on impact.

236 You are so dumb, when you dress up as a pirate you put a patch over both eyes.

237 You are so dumb you invented waterproof tea bags.

238 You are so dumb you invented a one-way escalator.

239 You are so dumb you invented non-stick glue.

240 You are so dumb you invented a fly screen on a submarine.

241 You are so dumb you could be brainwashed with an eye-dropper.

242 You are so dumb you got hit by a parked car.

243 If someone offered you a penny for your thoughts, they'd expect some change.

244 You are so dumb you asked for a price check at the $2 shop.

245 'Whenever I go to the store, they shake my hand.'
'I expect it's to make sure you don't put it in the till.'

246 I would ask you how old you are but I know you can't count that high.

247 'You'll just have to give me credit.'
'Well, I certainly won't be giving you cash.'

248 When Wally Witherspoon proposed to his girlfriend, she said, *'I love the simple things in life, Wally, but I don't want one of them for a husband!'*

249 I'm not being rude, you're just insignificant.

250 You are so dumb, when you went shoplifting you stole a free sample.

251 You are so dumb you called the 24-hour supermarket to see when they closed.

252 You're a miracle of nature. You have an IQ of 2 and you're still able to speak.

253 You are so dumb, when you missed the 44 bus you took the 22 twice instead.

254 You are so tight with your money you sit at the back of the bus to get a longer ride for your money.

255 You are so dumb, you saw a sign outside a police station that read 'Man Wanted for Robbery', and went in and applied for the job!

256 You are so dumb you leapt from a window to try out your new jumpsuit.

257 Instead of drinking from the fountain of knowledge, you just gargled.

258 How many toes does an idiot have?
Take off your socks and count them.

259 You are so dumb you kept banging your head against the wall because it felt so good when you stopped.

260 You are lower than the fluff in an earthworm's belly button.

261 Don't you have a terribly empty feeling – in your skull?

262 Every time you open your mouth your foot falls out.

263 He has a mind like a steel trap – always closed!

264 Jack: *'Mum, all the boys at school call me Big Head.'*
Mum: *'Never mind, dear, just run down to the grocery store and collect the big bag of apples I ordered in your cap.'*

265 If you stand close enough to him you can hear the ocean.

266 You would be out of your depth in a puddle.

267 Every time I take my girlfriend out for a meal, she eats her head off.
She looks better that way.

268 My girlfriend talks so much that when she goes to the beach she has to spread suntan lotion on her tongue!

269 He loves his wife so much, not only did he put in a swimming pool, he even bought a shark to go in it.

270 He's such a loser his bride turned up with a date on their wedding day.

271 I'd love to go out with you, but my favourite commercial is on TV.

272 I hear the only place you're ever invited to go is outside.

273 'I love looking in the mirror admiring my looks. Do you think that's vanity?'
'No, just a vivid imagination.'

274 I'll never forget the first time we met – although I keep trying.

275 'He's a boon to the whole area.'
'More like a baboon.'

276 'If we get married do you think you'll be able to live on my income?'
'Yes, but what will you live on?'

277 You can always spot my boyfriend at a party. Look for two people talking, and if one looks bored, then the other is my boyfriend.

278 'My boyfriend whispers that he loves me.'
'Well, it's not the sort of thing that he'd admit out loud.'

279 I wouldn't say you were hard-hearted but if I kicked you in the heart I'd break my foot.

280 'My girlfriend says that if I don't give up golf, she'll leave me.'
'Say, that's tough, old man.'
'Yeah, I'm going to miss her . . .'

281 Did your parents ever ask you to run away from home?

282 As an outsider, what do you think of the human race?

283 Anyone who told you to be yourself couldn't have given you worse advice.

284 When you were born your mother did not know which end to put the nappy on.

285 Are you just visiting this planet?

286 I don't know what your problem is, but I bet there's no cure.

287 Some day you will find yourself – and wish you hadn't.

288 You're not acting like yourself lately. I noticed the improvement immediately.

289 You remind me of a toenail. The sooner you get cut down to size the better.

290 You're a legend in your own mind!

291 Do you want people to accept you as you are or do you want them to like you?

292 Do you still love nature, despite what it did to you?

293 You are so dumb you tripped over a cordless phone.

294 Your sewing machine is out of thread.

295 You look lost in your thoughts – unfamiliar territory for you.

296 Are you always this stupid or are you making a special effort today?

297 So a thought crossed your mind? Must have been a long and lonely journey.

298 You are so dumb you planted coins in your garden because you wanted to raise some hard cash.

299 Your antenna isn't picking up all the channels.

300 I'm busy now. Can I ignore you some other time?

301 Everyone calls you 'Fog' because you are dense and wet.

302 You don't know the meaning of the word 'fear', but then again you don't know the meaning of most words.

303 With you here, your village must be missing its idiot.

304 You are like an oil well. Always boring.

305 Person 1: *'I've never been so insulted in all my life.'*
Person 2: *'You haven't been trying.'*

Tricky Tongue Twisters

Total twisters

1 Toy boat (this one looks easy, but say it ten times fast!)

2 Tongue twisters twist tongues.
Twisted tongues taste terrible.
Terrible tasting tongues
twist tightly.
A toast to tightly twisted terrible
tasting tongues.

3 The seventh ship sunk the sixth ship.

4 Active Adam asked Akmal for answers.

5 Tiny Tim thought trippy thoughts.

6 The fleeing fly finally flew fast.

7 Barry brought brilliant butter.
'Better bring better butter, Betty!'
Barry bellowed.
Betty bawled, berating Barry for
bringing better butter.
'Bother,' Betty's brother blackly
breathed.

8 'Sure, Samantha,' shy Shelley
said shyly.
She certainly shook and seemed
to shimmy.
Samantha smiled and served
shanks.
'Thanks,' said Shelley.

9 Four frozen flies were free to flee.

10 Sally's sore sore sure was sore.

11 Sammie spent six Saturdays slouching silently on the sofa.

12 Black background, brown background, blue background.

13 The thick, slippery snake sneaked and slithered.

14 Red lorries, yellow lollies.

15 Troy Boy bought Joy soy with joy.

16 Wally wore an Irish wristwatch. When wound, Wally's Irish wristwatch worked well.

17 In general, in January, Jenny generally generalised.

18 Wiley Wilma Wilmington was wilfully wilful.

19 The grinning gargoyle greedily gobbled green grapes.

20 The sleek, shiny shark swam silently.

21 An imaginary menagerie manager imagined managing many menageries.

22 Sleepy Sol soundly slept and loudly snored.

23 Wally wasn't really whimsical;
Wally wondered what
whimsical was.
Witty was what Wally wanted,
And witty was what Wally
resoundingly was.

24 Swiss watch, Swiss cheese.

25 Ordinarily, ordinary orange orangutans organised orderly outings.

26 The freezing freezer froze fast.
The fast freezing freezer
feels frozen.
The frozen freezer finally
defrosted.

27 Frieda's frantically funny face froze when the westerly wind wafted.

28 Mak met Mike; Mike met Mak;
Mike and Mak met Matt;
Mike, Mak and Matt met Mark;
Mike, Mak, Matt and Mark met Bob.

29 Sloppy Salina's slippers sadly slipped, sending Salina sliding and slipping.

30 Stewart slipped and tripped on the steep slope he trekked.

31 Both blue boats brought bait but borrowed Braydon's rods.

32 The stricken sinking sailor signalled SOS!

33 The porpoise purposely performed poetry on purpose.

34 The tired turtle tried to tread tenderly.

35 An accuser alleged Randal's actions as absolutely unacceptable.

36 Fearful Frankie thought fully frightening thoughts.

37 The big blue beanbag broke, blasting billions of beans backwards.

38 Right or wrong, white knights are right.

39 The poet poetically promised prime political poetry.

40 The sliding door silently slid softly shut.

41 The big, silver, shiny ship sank.

42 A particularly pleasant, playful Pop played pleasantly.

43 Left leg, right leg, red leg, yellow leg.

44 Every excellent egg easily excelled at exaggerating.

45 Harry hurriedly hopped happily.

46 Neil nearly kneeled nearby.

47 The awkward octopus awkwardly awoke.

48 Wendy whispered, Yanni yelled,
Ryan roared.
Wendy whispered, Yanni yelled,
Ryan roared.
Wendy roared, Yanni whispered,
Ryan yelled.
Wendy, Yanni, Ryan, yelled,
whispered, roared.

49 Pigeons surely shyly sit on statues.

50 Dripping tap, dip your hat.

51 Theoretically, the thirteenth shopfront shouldn't shut.

52 The drinking donkey drank delicately.

53 Faith faced faithfully west. Facing west, Faith faced friends fighting.

54 Cameron cruelly cut Christopher's crew cut, causing Christopher to cry.

55 The dog dragged Daisy's dolly for digging.

56 Larry liked licking yellow lollies.

57 Shane's shuttlecock shattered, sending Shane insane.

58 Bryan's a bald but buffed boxer.

That's gross!

59 A small, steamy smell silently slipped out.

60 Paul popped his pus-filled pimple.

61 Bob's big burp blasted barriers.

62 Really waxy ears are ringing.

63 Seth's breath smelled like death.

64 Ploppy Peter's pretty putridly pongy.

65 Suddenly, Samuel saw snotty Sarah stealing several strands of snot.

66 Sammy's sweaty shirt was soaked in sweat.
Silly Sally slipped on Sammy's sloppy sweat.
Simple Simon swam in Sammy's sweat.
Sammy simply said, 'That's wet.'

67 Frank's farts freaked Francine.

68 Eric's earwax was orange, obviously.

69 Flora's flatulence frighteningly floored Freddy.

70 Sweat-soaked smelly armpits stink.

71 My smelly, slimy, stinky sister's sloppy nappies.

72 Freddy's feet smelled foul.

73 Seth's stomach solemnly sent spew spewing.

74 Chucky's chunder had colourful carrot chunks.

75 Jerry's gorbies glowed green.

76 Doreen's double Dutch oven disgusted Darren.

77 Octavia's up-chuck was oddly orange.

78 Brock's B.O. brought Bob to tears.

79 Thick, slimy, sticky snot.

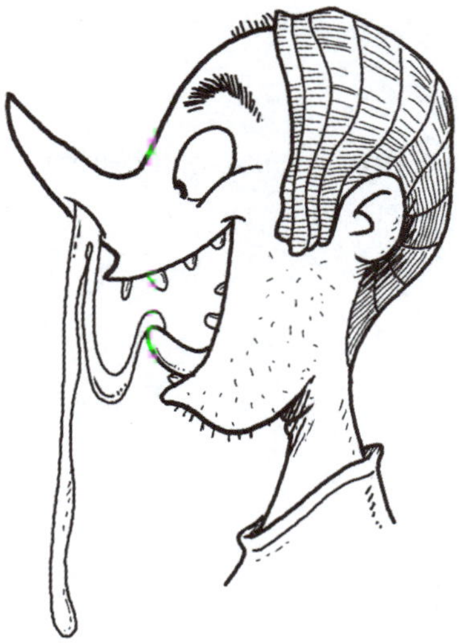

80 If Flora farted, Francine fell and Frannie fainted, how foul was Flora's fart?

81 The Queen quite cleverly created chaos with a steamy stinker.

82 Peter Popov popped off presently.

83 Orange spew, red spew, yellow spew, blue spew.

84 Four fighting farty fighters farted frequently while fighting ferociously.

Dinosaurs and cavemen

85 The tricky triceratops tripped a tyrannosaurus.

86 The spiky stegosaurus sipped a soda.

87 The brown brontosaurus borrowed bright but bland books.

88 The dopey dinosaur drank and dived and drowned.

89 Sixty-seven thick, thoughtless, sick stegosauruses stuck spikes in twenty-two trapped tyrannosauruses.

90 The creepy caveman crept quite creepily.

91 Warren wanted a real wheel to
do real wheelies;
What Warren really wanted was
a real wheel.
Warren wished wheels were real,
But for cavemen wheels
weren't real.

92 The terribly tiring pterodactyl was tragically trapped.

93 Stewie the stegosaurus slept
soundly;
Stewie the stegosaurus snored
solidly.

94 The fabulous fabrosaurus fabricated fabulously.

95 Bronwyn bathed the baby brontosaurus in blue bathwater.

96 A brachiosaurus bellowed with bronchitis.

What a monster!

97 The greedy giant ground bones.

98 A werewolf was really wary of rabies.

99 Frankenstein found France frustrating.

100 Horrid Harriet hated
Halloween.
Horrid Harriet found
Halloween harrowing.
Horrid Harriet had had it with
Halloween,
So Horrid Harriet holidayed in
Hawaii.

101 The Blob was a blobby gooey blob.

102 Seven short, slimy zombies sloshed, slipped and slid on a shiny, slippery slide.

103 Good ghosts generally greet guests jovially.

104 A werewolf's whiskers rarely waver.

105 Ghastly ghosts and grinning ghouls.

106 The alien alliance allowed acrobat eating.

107 A vampire thirstily sucked
thick blood.
He glugged, gobbled, gargled
and gulped,
He swished, swirled and
swallowed.

Marvellous magic

108 The sorcerer practised prickly imprisoning potions privately;
Practising privately perfected potions perfectly.

109 The wry wizard regularly worked on wand waving.

110 Which witch doctor rain danced?

111 Seth said six sick spells.
The six sick spells Seth said sent Sheldon's silliness soaring.
Silly Sheldon shouted sixty-six short spells.
The sixty-six short spells silly Sheldon shouted ensured Seth suddenly ceased saying sick spells.

112 A whacky wizard with white whiskers waved his wand.

113 Clara cleverly created classic card tricks.

114 Which wicked witch was wickedly wicked?

115 Wally wished he was a wizard.
Why did Wally wish for wizardry?
Really, what Wally wanted was really wicked wizard wear.

116 Trudy tried teaching Tyler trickery.

117 Casting and conjuring and creating confusion,
Illuminating and inventing and instigating illusion.

118 Michael's mighty mystical magic manipulated Maxine.

Let's get physical

119 Tony tried Terry's treadmill.

120 A broad bloke boxed blindly.

121 Peggy Babcock puffed and panted in pump class.

122 Darren dropped a dumbbell on his dad.

123 Sarah's sixth cycling session surely sucked.

124 Sandy surely showed super cycling style.

125 Brad's bulging biceps burst.

126 Tim took training tips and the training tips Tim took taught Tim to train.

127 Barbara's barbed-wire barbell.

128 Biceps, triceps, thigh sets, high reps.

129 Sandy skipped swiftly.

130 Six hundred and sixty-seven sit-ups sent sick Steve spewing.

131 Push-ups, press-ups, pull-ups, sit-ups.

132 Floundering Freya felt the burn.

Musical mayhem

133 Patiently practise picking, plucking, playing guitar.

134 Peter played pretty perfect piano.

135 Greg's grimy gooey green glockenspiel.

136 Ten trumpeters triumphantly trumpeted.

137 Princess Pauline, the pretty pianist, prettily played piano.

138 Ollie's orange organ.

139 Graham's groovy guitar grooves got Greg going gaga.

140 Trevor terribly trumpeted till Trixie trampled Trevor's trumpet.

141 Muriel miraculously made magical music.
Actually, Muriel's miraculously magical music was marvellous.

142 After the opera, Owen often opted for orange juice.

143 The brilliant big brass band played beautifully.

144 The string section suddenly went on strike, sending shockwaves shooting through the symphony.

145 Violent violinist.

146 The drummer dumbly decided to drum at dawn.

147 Brad's bassoon broke, bruising Brad badly.

148 Morose music makes Margaret mournful.

149 High notes, low notes, fast notes, slow notes, loud notes, soft notes, big nose, no nose.

150 Simon sang several sweet-sounding songs.

151 The crazy composer caused chaos, creating cringe-worthy compositions.

152 The orchestra owner often ordered octopus after eight.

153 Priscilla's pleasant piano playing perked up Paula.

154 Kelly cheered Klaus's classical symphonic composition.

155 Gloria's glockenspiel gently glowed and glimmered.

156 Trevor's triangle tinkled and tingled.

Fantasy that!

157 Slick Trixie, the tricky pixie, picked sticks.

158 Grant the giant generally jogged gratefully.

159 Bread grinding bones.

160 The braggin', arrogant, boastin' dragon.

161 The gabbling, gargling goblin gobbled and gargled.

162 Five fairies flipped five flapjacks.

163 Mermaids mainly mingle in lagoons.

164 Fourteen fickle fairies failed flying.

165 Eleven excited elves eagerly exited.

166 A pixie presently picked a perfect present.

167 Mallory the mermaid mostly made mischief.

168 The selfish elf ate shellfish.

What's cooking?

169 Sally's slippery serving spoon slipped while serving salad.

170 Frank frustratingly flipped forks. Frank's fork finally ferociously flipped.

171 Greg's gluggy gravy got gloopy.

172 Four flattened French fries.

173 Samantha slipped on thick,
sloppy sauce.
The kitchen cutlery clattered
and clunked.

174 Arthur halved hairy Harry's hash brown.

175 Silly Susan stirred a saucepan of spicy, steaming spinach soup with a spatula.

176 Greasy, grimy grills gladdened Gareth.

177 Practise proper pancake preparation to promise pristinely prepared perfect pancakes.

178 Corey's cooking class clapped Cara's crumble.

179 The chunky chef got charred cooking.

School days

180 Danny's detention definitely dragged.

181 Teaching trigonometry is tricky.

182 Sally spelled six synonyms.

183 Recess rocks!

184 Sick Steven skipped school.

185 Clara took glasses in cases to classes.
Clara carelessly cracked glasses in classes.
Clara's cracked glasses in cases in classes caused chaos.

186 Truant Tracey's truancy tricked teachers.

187 Steven's lunch bag seriously stank.

188 The maths course was massively maths based.

189 Elizabeth Hanson studied studiously.

190 Adam's attempted arithmetic answers were always error-riddled.

191 Geography is generally geographic.

192 Henrietta's horribly hard history homework was hysterical.

193 Frank finally passed physics after frequently failing.

194 Sirius's sister's slackness ensured slowly slipping science scores.

195 Peter played politely in the playground at playtime.

196 Leroy liked learning literature.

197 Cheating Cameron continuously copied Chelsea till checking teachers caught Cameron cheating, causing Cameron to cop a caning.

198 Trudy was tardy attending trigonometry; trigonometry truly was a trial for Trudy.

199 Aaron, Alex and Arwin arrived at after-school care all alone.

200 Suspension, expulsion, detention, yard duty.

201 Leisel learned lots of lessons at lunchtime.

202 The assistant principal's announcement signalled silence.

203 Steven suddenly stopped serious science study.

Silly sports

204 Shot-puts squash feet.

205 Wrestlers wearing Lycra are really weird.

206 Relay runners run relays really regularly.

207 The good golfer's green golf glove.

208 Prince Paul played polo pretty poorly.

209 Brandon's black boxing gloves broke bashing punching bags.

210 Twenty tenors tried tennis.

211 Stanley loved sitting, sipping soda on his sofa, seeing stunned skiers stacking in snow.
Seriously, Stanley loved seeing sporting slip-ups.

212 The golfer gripped the golf grip grudgingly.

213 The quick quiet cricketer requested cricketing competition.

214 The wild, wide wrestler went whacko.

215 The fighters frightened fans fighting a frightfully fearsome fight.

216 Callum's karate class created classic karate kicks.

217 The tenth table tennis championship challenge.

218 Paul played plinky, plonky ping-pong.

219 The athletes decided to discuss discus delegation.

220 Bobby the baseballer briefly broke baseball bats by bashing baseballs.

221 Athletic athletes are, at least, athletically athletic.

222 Sprinting Sally hurdled hurdles.

223 Boris beat Barney in breaststroke.

224 Right hook, left hook, uppercut, left jab.

225 Trevor's trophy for table tennis triumph was terrific.

226 Skeeter's skiing school skied slowly.

227 Bree's billiards brilliance bewildered Brooke.

228 Wayne likes white-water rafting after work.

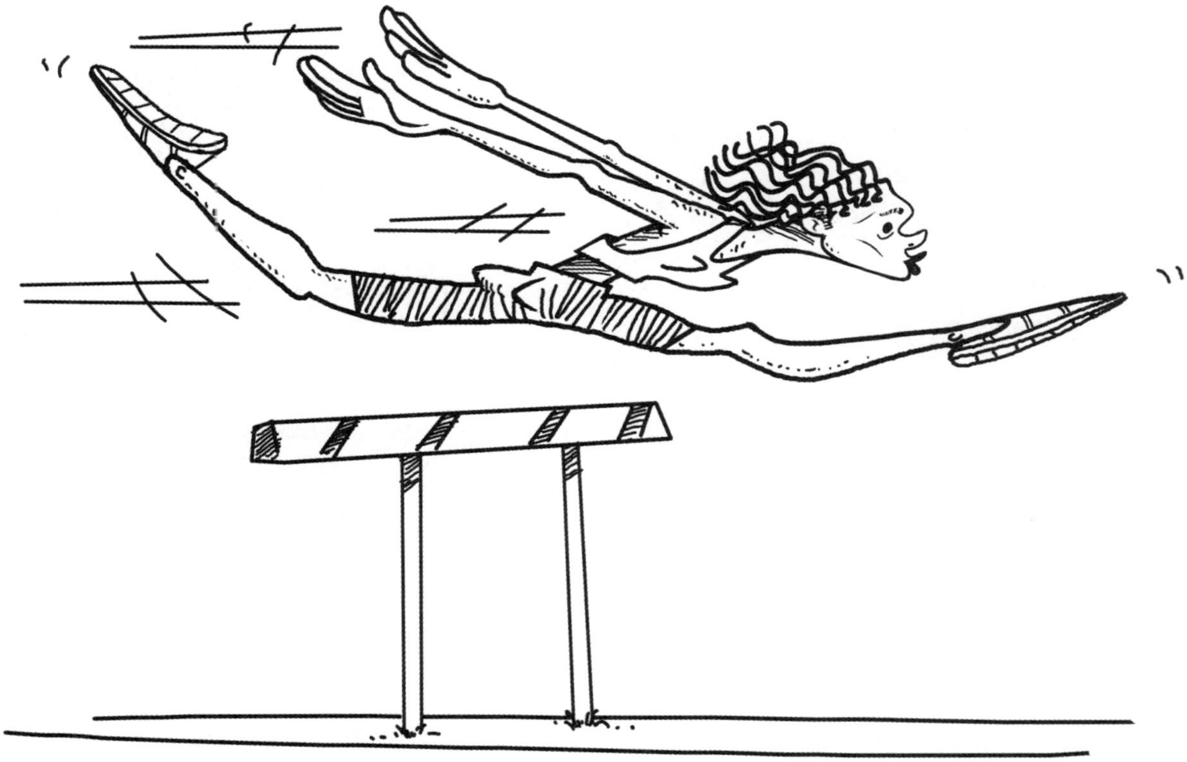

On the job

229 Chiropractors crack.

230 The pretty plumber perfected pipe work pretty perfectly.

231 Clare the carpenter quit carpentry quietly.

232 The doctor dictated a disease diagnosis delicately.

233 Harry's hammer hammered hurriedly.

234 Gary the gluer grimly gripped the glue gun.

235 The cheeky chef chose a chemist.

236 The bricklayer laid black bricks;
The bricklayer's bad black bricks broke.
Broken bricks bring bad news;
Broken bricks make bricklayers bankrupt.

237 The drunken, drear, dozy dentist drilled deeply.

238 Installing intricate interior insulation is easy.

239 The physical physiotherapist's therapy was fearful.

240 Sam stole stationery.

Funny animals

241 A hippy, hoppy, clippy, cloppy, undone zippo hippo.

242 A squishy, wishy, moshy, dishy, washy fishy.

243 A grabby, dabby, crabby, baby crab.

244 A wipy, stripy, swipy, gripy tiger.

245 A skinny, funny, spinny bunny.

246 A wordy, sturdy, nerdy, purdy birdie.

247 A tippy, tappy, snippy, clippie, sloppy, snappy alligator.

248 A punky, drunky, funky, clunky, cranky monkey.

249 A wizzy, dizzy, buzzy, fuzzy, fizzy fly.

250 An acrobatty, fatty, chitty, chatty, splatty, spitty gnat.

251 A barky, gawky, snarky, parky shark.

252 A wimpy, skimpy, clumpy, limpy, lumpy, bumpy chimpy.

253 A flippy, floppy, fancy, flicky French frog.

Twisted creatures

254 Andrew the ant-eating armadillo.

255 Domingo the flamingo.

256 Garret squawked, sang and swung.

257 Pat's buck-toothed babies had rabies.

258 Guy buzzed high like a fly.

259 Cecil the snake was slippery, slimy, scaly and sneaky.

260 Gerard the gazelle generally jauntily jumped.

261 Cherry the cheetah cheekily cheated.

262 Scott the skunk's skateboarding stunk.

263 Percy the platypus was a playful pet.

264 Sienna the shark swiftly swam southward.

265 Leo the lion lay lazily in the library.

Ahoy, maties!

266 Several cannon shots sunk six ships;
The seventh ship surprisingly set sail swiftly.
Pillaging pirates pursued, pillaged and plundered.

267 The flying skull and crossbones flag freely fluttered.

268 Peter's private pirate eye patch was pink.

269 Captain Crook's hook was quite curvy.

270 Captain Coronicus cleverly clapped creatively.

271 The first mate felt fully fine before he felt foul and fell ill.

272 Playing pirates placed Paula, Phil and Paul in fearful peril.

273 'Ensure the ship's shipshape for shore!'
'Sure, sir, the ship's sure in shipshape shape sir.'

274 The shipshape ship sailed slowly.

275 Previously, the pirate perilously perched on the precipice of the plank.
Presently, punishing pirates pressured, poked and pushed the pirate. Splash!

276 Skull and crossbones flag.

277 I live on a pirate ship.
(Think it's easy? Say it holding onto your tongue!)

Guts and gore

278 Crushed guts, guts crushed, crushed guts.

279 Blowfly-filled fluffy croissants.

280 Steven sliced Stewart with a sword.

281 Big black bugs bit Bryan;
Bryan's bites bled brilliantly.
Bad big black bugs!
Bryan's blue bazooka blasted big black bugs.

282 Blood-splattered pavement.

283 The white frothy rabid rat.

284 Simon screamed at scary sights: Nerve-wracking nightmares every night.

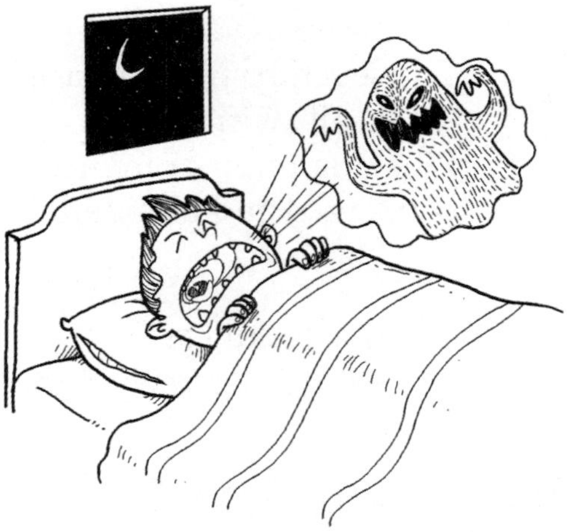

285 Jack Pratt, truck, 'duck!', Jack splat, Jack's flat, that's that.

286 Charlie's chainsaw chopped, sliced and diced.

287 Santo's sword severely severed Stanley.

288 Chop, cut, hack, slice, saw, sever, mince, dice.

289 Bill's broken bones brought black and blue bruising.

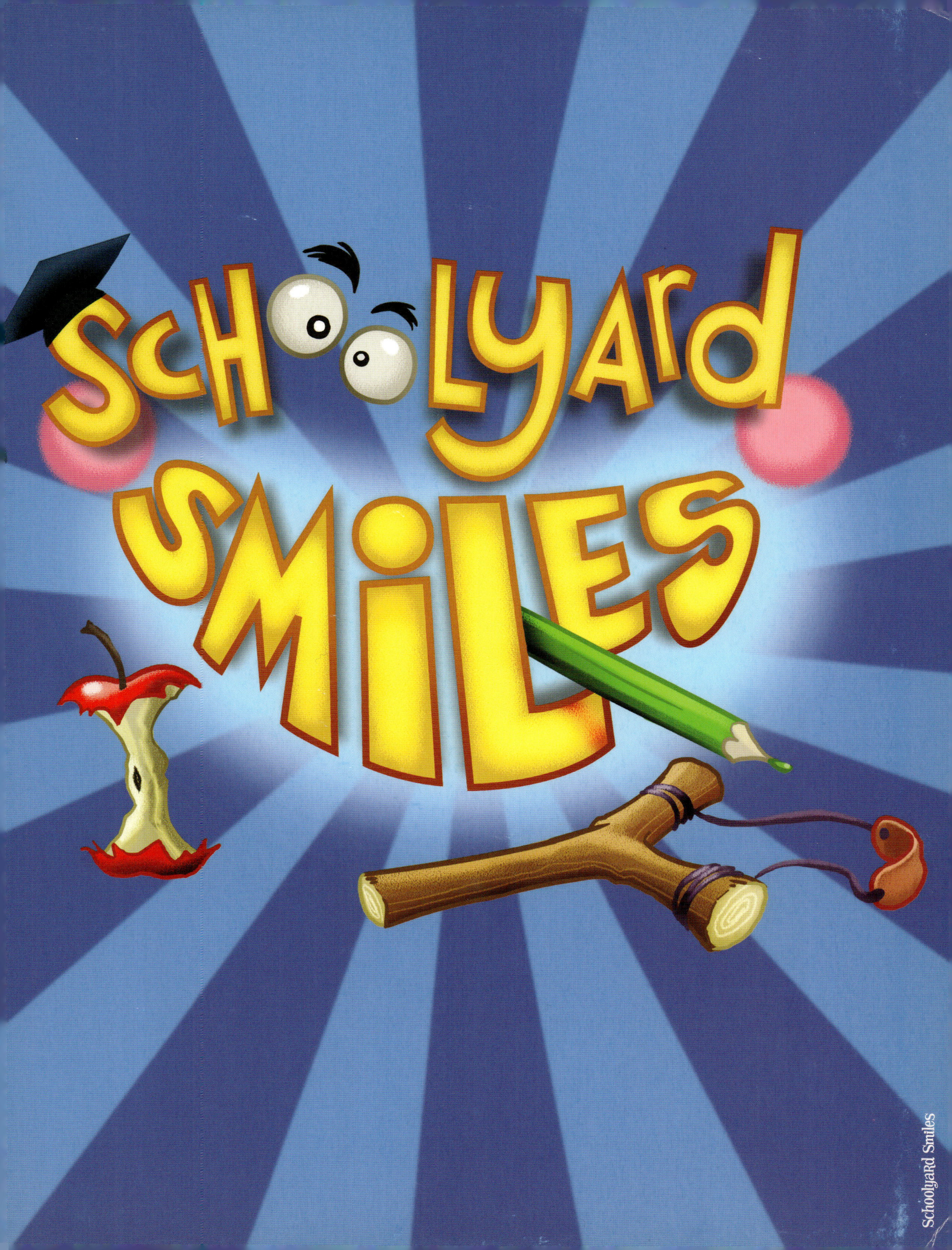

Schoolyard Smiles

1 Did you hear about the girl who got her brother a birthday cake, but then couldn't figure out how to get the cake in the typewriter to write 'Happy Birthday'?

2 English teacher: *'James, give me a sentence with the word "counterfeit" in it.'*
James: *'I wasn't sure if she was a centipede or a millipede, so I had to count her feet.'*

3 English teacher: *'Jamie, give me a sentence beginning with "I".'*
Jamie: *'I is …'.*
Teacher: *'No Jamie, you must always say "I am".'*
Jamie: *'Okay. I am the ninth letter of the alphabet.'*

4 Which dinosaur does well in English exams?
Tyrannathesaurus rex.

5 What language do birds speak?
Pigeon English.

6 How many letters are in the alphabet?
Eleven. Count them -t-h-e-a-l-p-h-a-b-e-t!

7 Mum: *'What are you doing, son?'*
Boy: *'Writing my brother a letter.'*
Mum: *'That's a lovely idea, but why are you writing so slowly?'*
Boy: *'Because he can't read very fast!'*

8 When Dad came home, he was amazed to see his son sitting on a horse, writing something. *'What are you doing up there?'* he asked.
'Well, the teacher told us to write an essay on our favourite animal,' replied the boy.

9 What word is always spelled wrong?
Wrong.

10 Did you hear about the student who said he couldn't write an essay about goldfish because he didn't have any waterproof ink?

11 My teacher says I've got such bad handwriting that I ought to be a doctor!

12 Maths teacher: *'Richard, if you had 50 cents in each trouser pocket, and $2 in each blazer pocket, what would you have?'*
Richard: *'Someone else's uniform, Sir.'*

13 *'How old would you say I am, Francis?'* the teacher asked.
'Forty,' said the boy promptly.
'What makes you think I'm forty?' asked the puzzled teacher.
'My big brother is twenty,' he replied, *'and you're twice as silly as he is!'*

14 Maths teacher: *'Anne, why have you brought a picture of the queen of England with you today?'*
Anne: *'You told us to bring a ruler with us.'*

15 Why are maths teachers good at solving detective stories?
Because they know when all the clues add up.

16 Maths teacher: *'If you multiplied 1386 by 395, what would you get?'*
Student: *'The wrong answer.'*

17 How does a maths teacher know how long she sleeps?
She takes a ruler to bed.

18 Why was the head teacher worried?
Because there were so many rulers in the school.

19 Did you hear about the maths teacher who wanted to order pizza for dinner, but was divided about whether to have additional cheese?

20 Teacher: *'Are you good at arithmetic?'*
Mary: *'Well, yes and no.'*
Teacher: *'What do you mean, yes and no?'*
Mary: *'Yes, I'm no good at arithmetic.'*

21 Which animals are best at maths?
Rabbits, because they're always multiplying.

22 There are three kinds of people in the world. Those who can count. And those who can't.

23

Teacher: *'If you had one dollar and asked your dad for one dollar, how much money would you have?'*
Student: *'One dollar.'*
Teacher: *'You don't know your maths.'*
Student: *'You don't know my dad!'*

24

Teacher: *'If I bought 100 buns for a dollar, what would each bun be?'*
Student: *'Stale.'*

25

Maths teacher: *'Paul. If you had five pieces of chocolate and Sam asked for one of them, how many would you have left?'*
Paul: *'Five.'*

26

Dad: *'How did you find your maths exam?'*
Son: *'Unfortunately, it wasn't lost!'*

27

Principal: *'You should have been here at 9.00.'*
Student: *'Why, what happened?'*

28

Student: *'I don't think I deserve a zero on this test.'*
Teacher: *'No, neither do I but it was the lowest I could give you!'*

29

Why did the boy throw his watch out of the window during an exam?
Because he wanted to make time fly.

30

Father: *'I want to take my girl out of this terrible maths class.'*
Teacher: *'But she's top of the class!'*
Father: *'That's why it must be a terrible class!'*

31

Teacher: *'I hope I didn't see you copying from John's exam paper, James.'*
James: *'I hope you didn't see me either!'*

32

How do you make seven an even number?
Take off the s.

33

'I hope you're not one of those boys who sits and watches the school clock,' said the principal to the new boy.
'No, Sir,' he replied. *'I've got a digital watch that beeps at three-fifteen!'*

34 Teacher: *'What family does the octopus belong to?'*
Student: *'Nobody's I know.'*

35 Science teacher: *'Which travels faster, heat or cold?'*
Student: *'Heat, because you can catch a cold.'*

36 Student 1: *'We bought our retiring science teacher a gift – toilet water that cost $20.'*
Student 2: *'What! I would've sold you water from our toilet for only $2!'*

37 In which class do you learn how to shop for bargains?
Buy-ology.

38 What do you do with crude oil?
Teach it some manners.

39 Teacher: *'What's the name of a liquid that won't freeze?'*
Student: *'Hot water.'*

40 What type of music do geologists like best?
Rock.

41 Science teacher: *'What are nitrates?'*
Student: *'Cheaper than day rates.'*

42 Big brother: *'That planet over there is Mars.'*
Little brother: *'Then that other one must be Pa's.'*

43 Student: *'Where can I find out about ducks?'*
Librarian: *'Try the ducktionary.'*

44 When did the last dinosaur die?
After the second-last dinosaur.

45 Computer teacher: *'Sarah, give me an example of software.'*
Sarah: *'A floppy hat.'*

46 'Do you turn on your computer with your left hand or your right hand?'
'My right hand.'
'Amazing! Most people have to use the on/off switch!'

47 Doctor, Doctor, my little brother thinks he's a computer.
Well bring him in so I can cure him.
I can't, I need to use him to finish my homework!

48 Parent: *'In my day we didn't have computers at school to help us.'*
Child: *'You mean you got your schoolwork wrong all on your own?'*

49 Did you hear about the technology teacher who left teaching to try to make something of himself?

50 What is the robot teacher's favourite part of the day?
Assembly.

51 How do you know when a spider is cool?
It has its own website.

52 Why did the cat sit on the computer?
To keep an eye on the mouse.

53 'Mum, Mum, Dad's broken my computer!'
'How did he do that?'
'I dropped it on his head!'

54 'Is that the computer help line? Every time I log on to the Seven Dwarves website, my computer screen goes snow white . . .'

55 What do you get when you cross an overheating Apple computer with fast food?
A Big Mac and fries.

56 History teacher: *'Why do we refer to the period around 1000 years AD as the Dark Ages?'*
Student: *'Because there were so many knights.'*

57 History teacher: *'What's the best thing about history?'*
Mary: *'All the dates.'*

58 History teacher: *'What was Camelot?'*
Student: *'A place where camels were parked.'*

59 History teacher: *'Here is a question to check that you did your homework on British kings and queens. Who came after Mary?'*
Student: *'Her little lamb.'*

60 History teacher: *'Why were ancient sailing ships so eco-friendly?'*
Student: *'Because they could go for hundreds of miles to the galleon.'*

61 History teacher: *'What's a Grecian urn?'*
Student: *'About $500 a week.'*

62 Did you hear about the two history teachers who were dating?
They go to restaurants to talk about old times.

63 Did you hear about the school kid who was studying Greek mythology?
When the teacher asked him to name something that was half-man and half-beast he replied, 'Buffalo Bill'.

64 Why was the Egyptian girl worried?
Because her Daddy was a Mummy!

65 What type of instruments did the early Britons play?
The Anglo-saxophone.

66 Where did Noah keep the bees?
In the ark hives.

67 Teacher: *'What came after the Stone Age and the Bronze Age?'*
Student: *'The saus-age.'*

68 What are the names of the small rivers that run into the Nile?
The juve-niles.

69 Geography teacher: *'What's the coldest country in the world?'*
Student: *'Chile.'*

70 Where is the English Channel?
Not sure. It's not on my TV.

71 Name three famous poles.
North, south and tad.

72 What birds are found in Portugal?
Portu-geese.

73 What do you know about the Dead Sea?
Dead? I didn't even know it was sick!

74 Mother: *'Did you get a good place in the geography test?'*
Daughter: *'Yes, I sat next to the cleverest kid in the class.'*

75 Simple Simon was writing a geography essay for his teacher. It began like this:
The people who live in Paris are called parasites.

76 Name an animal that lives on the tundra.
A reindeer.
Name another.
Another reindeer.

77 Why is the Mississippi such an unusual river?
It has four eyes and can't even see.

78 Do you know where to find elephants?
Elephants don't need finding – they're so big they don't get lost.

79 What's the tallest yellow flower in the world?
A giraffodil.

80 'Do you think, Professor, that my girlfriend should take up the piano as a career?'
'No, I think she should put down the lid as a favour!'

81 How many aerobics teachers does it take to change a light bulb?
Five, one to change it, the others to say, 'A Little to the left, a little to the right, a little to the left, a little to the right.'

82 What do you get when you cross a plumber with a ballerina?
A tap dancer.

83 Where do footballers dance?
At a football!

84 Have you heard about the gym teacher who ran around exam rooms, hoping to jog students' memories?
. . . Or, the craft teacher who had her pupils in stitches?
. . . Or, maybe, the cookery teacher who thought Hamlet was an omelette with bacon?

85 Teacher to parent: *'David's career choice as a train driver will suit him well. He has more experience of lines than any other student at this school!'*

86 When George left school he was going to be a printer.
All his teachers said he was the right type.

87 Why was the musician in prison?
Because he was always getting into treble.

88 What do you call an art teacher who is always complaining?
Mona Lisa.

89 Cookery teacher: *'Helen, what are the best things to put in a fruit cake?'*
Helen: *'Teeth!'*

90 Why wasn't the butterfly invited to the dance?
Because it was a moth ball.

91 Student: *'Would you punish someone for something they didn't do?'*
Teacher: *'Of course not.'*
Student: *'Good, because I didn't do my homework.'*

92 Shane: *'Dad, today my teacher yelled at me for something I didn't do.'*
Dad: *'What did he yell at you for?'*
Shane: *'For not doing my homework.'*

93 Girl to friend: *'I'm sorry, I won't be able to come out tonight. I promised Dad I'd stay in and help him with my homework.'*

94 What do you call someone who greets you at the school door every morning?
Matt.

95 Why can you believe everything a bearded teacher tells you?
They can't tell bare-faced lies.

96 Student: *'I didn't do my homework because I lost my memory.'*
Teacher: *'When did this start?'*
Student: *'When did what start?'*

97 What's the difference between a train station and a teacher?
One minds the train, the other trains the mind.

98 Did you hear about the teacher who locked the school band in a deep freeze?
They wanted to play really cool jazz.

99 Mother: *'I told you not to eat cake before supper.'*
Son: *'But it's part of my homework – see – if you take an eighth of a cake from a whole cake, how much is left?'*

100 Why did the student stand on his head?
To turn things over in his mind.

101 'Be sure to go straight home from school.'
'I can't – I live around the corner!'

102 Teacher: *'Tom, why are you late?'*
Tom: *'The train had a flat tyre.'*

103 Teacher: *'That's three times I've asked you a question. Why won't you reply?'*
Student: *'Because you told me not to answer you back.'*

104 *'What are three words most often used by students?'* the teacher asked the class.
'I don't know,' sighed a student.
'That's correct!' said the teacher.

105 First teacher: *'What's wrong with young Jimmy today? I saw him running around the playground, screaming and pulling at his hair.'*
Second teacher: *'Don't worry. He's just lost his marbles.'*

106 Teacher: *'I told you to stand at the end of the line.'*
Student: *'I tried, but there was someone already there.'*

107 Teacher: *'What's the name of a bird that doesn't build its own nest?'*
Student: *'The cuckoo.'*
Teacher: *'That's right – how did you know that?'*
Student: *'Easy, Sir, everyone knows cuckoos live in clocks!'*

108 Teacher: *'Why can't you answer any of my questions in class?'*
Student: *'If I could, there wouldn't be much point in me being here.'*

109 Teacher: *'I said to draw a cow eating grass, but you've only drawn a cow.'*
Student: *'Yes, the cow has eaten all the grass.'*

110 Teacher: *'That's the stupidest boy in the whole school.'*
Mother: *'That's my son.'*
Teacher: *'Oh! I'm so sorry.'*
Mother: *'You're sorry!'*

111 Teacher: *'Why didn't you answer me, Stuart?'*
Stuart: *'I did, I shook my head.'*
Teacher: *'You don't expect me to hear it rattling from here, do you?'*

112 Teacher: *'I wish you'd pay a little attention.'*
Student: *'I'm paying as little attention as possible.'*

113 Father: *'How do you like going to school?'*
Son: *'Going and coming home are fine; it's the part in the middle I don't like!'*

114 *'Do you like your new school, Billy?'* asked Uncle Ned.
'Sometimes,' said the boy.
'When is that?'
'When it's closed!'

115 What is the easiest way to get a day off school?
Wait until Saturday.

116 Teacher: *'You missed school yesterday, didn't you?'*
Student: *'Not very much.'*

117 *'Are you lost?'* the policeman asked the schoolgirl.
'Of course not,' she replied. 'I'm here, it's my school that's lost.'

118 The teacher told Jack he knew he'd skipped school last Friday, and heard he'd been playing at the games arcade.
Jack told him it wasn't true – and he had the football game tickets to prove it!

119 *'I'm not going to school today,'* said Alexander to his mother. *'The teachers bully me and the boys in my class don't like me. Why?'*
'Firstly, you're 35 years old,' replied his mother, *'and secondly, you're the principal!'*

120 'Mum, I'm not going to school today.'
'Why not?'
'Because it's Sunday.'

121 Playing truant from school is like having a credit card.
Lots of fun now, pay later.

122 Teacher: *'Why haven't you been to school for the last two weeks, Billy?'*
Billy: *'It's not my fault – whenever I go to cross the road outside, there's a man with a sign saying "Stop Children Crossing"!'*

123 Did you hear about the teacher who wore sunglasses to give out exam results?
He took a dim view of his students' performance.

124 Why did the teacher wear sunglasses?
Because his students were so bright.

125 Did you hear about the cross-eyed teacher?
He couldn't control his pupils.

126 'Our teacher talks to herself in class, does yours?'
'Yes, but she doesn't realise it. She thinks we're listening!'

127 Teacher: *'Billy, stop making ugly faces at the other students!'*
Billy: *'Why?'*
Teacher: *'Well, when I was your age, I was told that if I kept making ugly faces, my face would stay that way.'*
Billy: *'Well, I can see you didn't listen.'*

128 Teacher: *'I'd like you to be very quiet today, girls. I've got a dreadful headache.'*
Mary: *'Please Miss, why don't you do what Mum does when she has a headache?'*
Teacher: *'What's that?'*
Mary: 'She sends us out to play!'

129 *'What were you before you came to school, girls and boys?'* asked the teacher, hoping that someone would say 'babies'. She was disappointed when all the children cried out, *'Happy!'*

130 Teacher: *'Did you know the bell had gone?'*
Sue: *'I didn't take it, Miss.'*

131 Teacher: *'Sue, what letter comes after the letter A?'*
Sue: *'The rest of them.'*

132 Laugh, and the class laughs with you.
But you get detention alone.

133 Teacher: *'How was your holiday, Penny?'*
Penny: *'Great. My brother and I spent the whole time on the beach, burying each other in the sand.'*
Teacher: *'That sounds like fun.'*
Penny: *'Daddy says we can go back next year and find him.'*

134 Marco: *'My sister has lovely long hair, all down her back.'*
Will: *'Pity it's not on her head!'*

135 First boy: *'My brother said he'd tell me everything he knows.'*
Second boy: *'He must have been speechless!'*

136 First boy: *'Does your brother keep himself clean?'*
Second boy: *'Oh, yes, he takes a bath every month, whether he needs one or not!'*

137 Mary: *'Do you think my sister's pretty?'*
Tim: *'Well, let's just say if you pulled her pigtail, she'd probably say "oink, oink"!'*

138 Dan: *'My little brother is a real pain.'*
Nan: *'Things could be worse.'*
Dan: *'How?'*
Nan: *'He could be twins!'*

139 First boy: *'Why is your brother always flying off the handle?'*
Second boy: *'Because he's got a screw loose!'*

140 Did you hear about the time Eddie's sister tried to make a birthday cake?
The candles melted in the oven.

141 Why did your sister put her socks on inside out?
Because there was a hole on the outside.

142 Brother: *'What happened to you?'*
Sister: *'I fell off while I was riding.'*
Brother: *'Horseback?'*
Sister: *'I don't know. I'll find out when I get back to the stable.'*

143 Peter: *'My brother wants to work badly!'*
Anita: *'As I remember, he usually does!'*

144 Did you hear about the little boy who was named after his father?
They called him Dad.

145 Ben's teacher thinks Ben is a wonder child.
She wonders whether he'll ever learn anything.

146 George is the type of boy that his mother doesn't want him to hang around with . . .

147 Teacher: *'Your daughter's only five and she can spell her name backwards? Why, that's remarkable!'*
Mother: *'Yes, we're very proud of her.'*
Teacher: *'And what is your daughter's name?'*
Mother: *'Anna.'*

148 *'The girl who sits beside me in maths is very clever,'* said Alec to his mother. *'She has enough brains for two.'*
'Perhaps you'd better think of marriage,' said his mum.

149 Mum: *'Haven't you finished filling the salt shaker yet?'*
Son: *'Not yet. It's really hard to get the salt through all those little holes!'*

150 'Dad, can you write in the dark?'
'I suppose so.'
'Good. Can you sign my report card, please?'

151 Mum: *'How can you practise your trumpet and listen to the radio at the same time?'*
Son: *'Easy, I have two ears!'*

152 *'William, I've been told you tried to put paint on two boys at school,'* said his dad.
'Yes Dad,' said William.
'They are twins and I needed a way to tell them apart!'

153 Mum: *'Why are you scratching Jamie?'*
Jamie: *'Because no one else knows where I itch.'*

154 Why did your brother ask your father to sit in the freezer?
Because he wanted an ice-cold pop!

155 Jane: *'Do you like me?'*
Wayne: *'As girls go, you're fine . . . and the sooner you go, the better!'*

156 Roy: *'They say ignorance is bliss.'*
Rita: *'Then you should be the happiest boy in the world!'*

157 Why did your brother go to school at night?
Because he wanted to learn to read in the dark!

158 Dick and Jane were arguing over the breakfast table.
'Oh, you're so stupid!' shouted Dick.
'Dick!' said their father. *'That's quite enough! Now say you're sorry.'*
'Okay,' said Dick. *'Jane, I'm sorry you're stupid.'*

159 *'Alice, you never get anything right,'* complained the teacher. *'What kind of job do you think you'll get when you leave school?'*
'Well, I want to be a weather girl on TV,' said Alice.

160 Did you hear about the dizzy Boy Scout?
He spent all day doing good turns.

161 *'What shall we play today?'* Tanya asked her best friend, Emma.
'Let's play school,' said Emma.
'Okay,' said Tanya.
'But I'm going to be absent.'

162 Why did the boy take a pencil to bed?
To draw the curtains!

163 I'd tell you another joke about a boy and a pencil, but there's no point.

164 'I play Scrabble with my pet dog every night.'
'He must be clever.'
'I don't know about that. I usually beat him.'

165 Did you hear about the girl who wrote herself a letter but forgot to sign it?
When it arrived, she didn't know who it was from!

166 Emma: *'What a cool pair of odd socks you have on, Jill.'*
Jill: *'Yes, and I have another pair just like it at home.'*

167 *'Why are you crying, Ted?'* asked his mum.
'Because my new sneakers hurt,' Ted replied.
'That's because you've put them on the wrong feet.'
'But they're the only feet I have!'

168 First girl: *'Whenever I'm down in the dumps, I buy myself a new hat.'*
Second girl: *'Oh, so that's where you get them!'*

169 Why did the boy wear five watches?
He liked to have a lot of time on his hands.

170 Did you hear what Dumb Donald did when he offered to paint the garage for his dad?
The instructions said put on three coats – so he put on his jacket, his raincoat and his overcoat!

171 Why do we dress baby girls in pink and baby boys in blue?
Because babies can't dress themselves.

172 Why did the boy wear a life jacket in bed?
Because he slept on a waterbed.

173 What do you call a lion wearing a hat?
A dandy lion.

174 Why do doctors wear masks when operating?
Because if they make a mistake, no one will know who did it!

175 Did you hear about the girl who was so keen on road safety that she always wore white at night?
Last winter she was knocked down by a snow plough.

176 My big brother is such an idiot. The other day I saw him hitting himself over the head with a hammer.
He was trying to make his head swell, so his hat wouldn't fall over his eyes!

177 George knocked on the door of his friend's house. When his friend's mother answered he asked,
'Can Albert come out to play?'
'No,' said Albert's mother.
'It's too cold.'
'Well then,' said George, *'can his football come out to play?'*

178 Dad: *'Don't be selfish. Let your brother use the sled half the time.'*
Son: *'I do, Dad. I use it going down the hill and he gets to use it coming up the hill!'*

179 First girl: *'Why are you putting your horse's saddle on backward?'*
Second girl: *'How do you know which way I'm going?'*

180 Why did Matt's bicycle keep falling over?
Because it was two-tyred.

181 What did the football player say when he accidentally burped during the game?
'Sorry, it was a freak hic!'

182 Why do artists never win when they play basketball?
They keep drawing!

183 'I played Beethoven last night.'
'Who won?'

184 Why didn't the dog want to play football?
It was a boxer!

185 How did the basketball court get wet?
The players dribbled all over it!

186 How do hens encourage their football teams?
They egg them on!

187 A boy broke his arm playing football. After his arm had been put into a cast, he asked the doctor, *'When you take the plaster off, will I be able to play the drums?'*
'Of course you will,' said the doctor, reassuringly.
'That's great!' said the boy. *'I've never been able to play before!'*

188 A girl walked into a pet shop and said, *'I'd like a frog for my brother.'*
'Sorry,' said the shopkeeper. *'We don't do exchanges!'*

189 One day Joe's mother said to his father, *'It's such a nice day, I think I'll take Joe to the zoo.'*
'I wouldn't bother,' said his father. *'If they want him, let them come and get him!'*

190 Dad was taking Danny around the museum, when they came across a magnificent stuffed lion in a case.
'Dad,' asked a puzzled Danny, *'how did they shoot the lion without breaking the glass?'*

191 What is a polygon?
A dead parrot.

192 Did you hear about the boy who sat under a cow?
He got a pat on the head.

193 Little brother: *'I'm going to buy a seahorse.'*
Big brother: *'Why?'*
Little brother: *'Because I want to play water polo!'*

194 Where would you weigh a whale?
At a whale-weigh station.

195 Which bird can lift the heaviest weights?
The crane.

196 'I've lost my dog.'
'Put an ad in the paper.'
'Don't be silly. He can't read.'

197 *'Mary,'* said her teacher, *'you can't bring that lamb into class. What about the smell?'*
'Oh, that's all right Miss,' replied Mary. *'It'll soon get used to it.'*

198 How do dinosaurs pass exams?
With extinction.

199 Why doesn't your sister like peanuts?
Have you ever seen a skinny elephant?

200 Why did the lazy boy get a job in a bakery?
Because he wanted to loaf around!

201 Which king was purple and had many wives?
King Henry the Grape.

202 Girl: *'How much is a soft drink?'*
Waitress: *'Fifty cents.'*
Girl: *'How much is a refill?'*
Waitress: *'The first is free.'*
Girl: *'Well then, I'll have a refill.'*

203 Lucy: *'If you eat any more ice-cream, you'll burst.'*
Lindy: *'Okay – pass the ice-cream and duck.'*

204 What's purple, 5000 years old and 400 kilometres long?
The Grape Wall of China.

205 Did you hear about the boy who stole some rhubarb?
He was put into custardy.

206 Have you ever seen a man-eating tiger?
No, but in a restaurant next door I once saw a man eating chicken . . .

207 Two girls were having lunch in the school yard. One had an apple, and the other said, *'Watch out for worms, won't you!'*
The first girl replied, *'Why should I? They can watch out for themselves!'*

208 Penny: *'Will you join me in a cup of hot chocolate?'*
Mindy: *'Yes, but do you think we'll both fit?'*

209 'My brother's been practising the violin for ten years.'
'Is he any good?'
'No, it was nine years before he found out he wasn't supposed to blow!'

210 'Our Jackie learnt to play the violin in no time at all.'
'So I can hear.'

211 Why did Silly Sue throw her guitar away?
Because it had a hole in the middle.

212 A little boy came home from his first day at kindergarten and said to his mother, *'What's the use of going to school? I can't read, I can't write, and the teacher won't let me talk!'*

213 Dad: *'Why is your January progress report so bad?'*
Son: *'Well, you know how it is. Things are always marked down after Christmas!'*

214 Why did the girl separate the thread from the needle?
Because the needle had something in its eye.

215 Why did the girl cut a hole in her new umbrella?
Because she wanted to tell when it stopped raining!

216 *'Mum,'* Richard yelled from the kitchen. *'You know that dish you were always worried I'd break?'*
'Yes dear, what about it?' said his mum.
'Well . . . your worries are over.'

217 A young boy was helping his dad around the house.
'Son, you're like lightning with that hammer,' said the father.
'Really fast, eh, Dad?' said the boy.
'No, Son. You never strike in the same place twice!'

218 Did you hear about the boy who had to do a project about trains?
He had to keep track of everything.

219 Visitor: *'You're very quiet, Louise.'*
Louise: *'Well, my mum gave me a dollar not to say anything about your red nose.'*

220 Did you hear about my brother? *He saw a moose's head hanging on a wall and went into the next room to find the rest of it!*

221 *'I think my Dad's getting taller,'* said Stan, to his friend.
'What makes you think that?'
'Well, lately I've noticed that his head is sticking through his hair.'

222 *'Mum, can I please change my name right now?'* asked Ben.
'Why would you want to do that, dear?' asked his mum.
'Because Dad says he's going to ground me, as sure as my name's Benjamin!'

223 Mother: *'Cathy, get your little sister's hat out of that puddle!'*
Cathy: *'I can't, Mum. She's got it strapped too tight under her chin.'*

224 Boy: *'Grandpa, do you know how to croak?'*
Grandpa: *'No, I don't. Why?'*
Boy: *'Because Daddy says he'll be a rich man when you do!'*

225 A scoutmaster asked a boy in his troop what good deed he had done that day.
'Well,' said the Scout. *'My Mum only had one chore left, so I let my brother do it.'*

226 Uncle Herbert noticed that his nephew Johnny was watching him all the time.
'Why are you always looking at me?' he asked.
'I was just wondering when you were going to do your trick,' replied Johnny.
'What trick?' asked Uncle Herbert.
'Well, Mum says you eat like a horse . . .'

227 *'Mum, there's a man at the door collecting for the Old Folks' Home,'* said the little boy. *'Shall I give him Grandma?'*

228 Why do elephants have trunks?
Because they can't fit everything into a handbag.

229 Where do elephants go on holidays?
Tuscany.

230 Why do buffaloes always travel in herds?
Because they're afraid of getting mugged by elephants.

231 Did you hear about the two boys who found themselves in a modern art gallery by mistake?
'Quick,' said one. *'Run, before they say we did it!'*

232 Mary's class went to the Natural History Museum.
'Did you enjoy yourself?' asked her mother, when she got home.
'Oh, yes,' replied Mary. *'But it was funny going to a dead zoo!'*

233 What do you call a travelling mosquito?
An itch hiker.

234 Where did the cow go for its holiday?
Moo Zealand.

235 *'I hope this plane doesn't travel faster than sound,'* said the girl to the flight attendant.
'Why?' asked the flight attendant. *'Because my friend and I want to talk, that's why!'*

236 Jane was telling her friend about her holiday in Switzerland. Her friend asked, *'What did you think of the beautiful scenery?'*
'Oh, I couldn't see much,' said Jane. *'There were too many mountains in the way.'*

237 We went for a holiday last year to a seaside town.
It was so boring there that the tide went out one day and didn't come back!

238 What's red, white and brown and travels faster than the speed of sound?
An astronaut's ham and tomato sandwich.

239 Two girls were talking in the corridor.
'That boy over there is getting on my nerves,' said Clare.
'But he's not even looking at you,' replied Megan.
'That's why he's getting on my nerves!' exclaimed Clare.

240 James: *'I call my girlfriend Peach.'* John: *'Because she's soft, and beautiful as a peach?'*
James: *'No, because she's got a heart of stone.'*

241 What are teenage giraffes told when they go on their first date?
No necking.

242 What did the boa constrictor say to its victim?
'I've got a crush on you.'

243 'I got a gold watch for my girlfriend.'
'I wish I could make a trade like that!'

244 What does every girl have that she can always count on?
Fingers.

245 Who were the world's shortest lovers?
Gnomeo and Juliet.

246 I can't understand why people say my girlfriend's legs look like matchsticks.
They do look like sticks – but they certainly don't match!

247 What do girl snakes write on the bottom of their letters?
With love and hisses!

248 What happened to the male bee that fell in love?
He got stuck on his honey.

249 What happened when the snowman girl had a fight with her boyfriend?
She gave him the cold shoulder.

250 *Keep on Trying* by Percy Vere

251 *Crossing Roads Safely* by Luke Bothways

252 *The Long Walk to School* by Mr Bus

253 *Getting Your Homework Done* by Mae B Tomorrow

254 *The Terrible Problem* by Major Setback

255 *Always Late* by Chester Minnit

256 *How to be Taller by* Stan Dupp

257 *How to be Shorter* by Neil Down

258 *World Atlas* by Joe Graffie

259 *Adding Up* by Juan and Juan

260 *Dealing With Bullies* by Howard U Lykett

261 *Speaking French* by Lorna Lang Wedge